THE
FINDHORN
BOOK OF

Forgiveness

by
Michael Dawson
author of *Healing the Cause – A Path of Forgiveness*

First published by Findhorn Press 2003

ISBN 1 84409 012 4

British Library Cataloguing-in-Publication Data.
A catalogue record for this book is available from the British Library.

Edited by Elaine Harrison
Cover and internal book design by Thierry Bogliolo
Cover background photograph and central photograph by Digital Vision

A Course In Miracles® is a registered trademark of the Foundation for A Course In Miracles,
Inc.® in United States and other countries. Findhorn Press is independent of the Foundation for A
Course In Miracles®. Portions from *A Course in Miracles*®1975, 1992, 1996 reprinted by permission
of the Foundation for A Course In Miracles, Inc.® (www.facim.org). All rights reserved. The ideas
represented herein are the personal understanding of the author and are not necessarily endorsed by the
copyright holder for *A Course in Miracles*®.
The poem *Refusal* is used with permission of its author, Minette Quick.
The excerpt from *Forgiveness and Jesus – The Meeting Place of "A Course in Miracles" and
Christianity* by Dr. Kenneth Wapnick © 1983 is used with permission of Foundation for A Course In
Miracles, 41397 Buecking Drive, Temecula, CA 92590 [www.facim.org]
The excerpt from *Return from Tomorrow* by George G. Ritchie, M.D. © 1978 is used
with permission of Fleming H. Revell, a division of Baker Book House Company.
The quotation from *The Power of Now* by Eckhart Tolle © 1997 is used
with permission of Namaste Publishing Inc., Vancouver.
The quotation from *And There Was Light — the autobiography of a blind hero in the French
Resistance* by Jacques Lusseyran © Estate of Jacques Lusseyran 1953, 1963 is used with permission of
Floris Books, Edinburgh.

Printed and bound by WS Bookwell, Finland

Published by

Findhorn Press

305a The Park, Findhorn
Forres IV36 3TE
Scotland, UK

tel 01309 690582 • fax 01309 690036
e-mail: info@findhornpress.com

findhornpress.com

CONTENTS

To my wife Elinor Drake
whose love, encouragement and editing skills
have been such a great support,
and to John Montgomery
for his friendship and ongoing demonstration of forgiveness.

ACKNOWLEDGEMENTS

I would like to acknowledge my indebtedness to Dr. Kenneth Wapnick whose books and tapes on *A Course in Miracles*® have been rich sources of teaching and inspiration. In particular his book *Forgiveness and Jesus – The Meeting Place of "A Course in Miracles" and Christianity* has been of particular value, especially in regard to the AAA Approach to Forgiveness in Chapter Four. He also kindly took time from his busy schedule to read and comment on my manuscript. Responsibility for the book's contents remains my own, however.

Throughout the writing of the book my wife Elinor Drake has been a constant source of encouragement and made many helpful observations. She has proof read the whole manuscript and maintained a critical eye on all aspects of the work.

I am grateful to Elaine Harrison in her role as Editor at Findhorn Press in providing many insightful observations, which has led to a clearer presentation of my material.

The inspiration for this book has come from *A Course in Miracles*®. After 20 years of study I never fail to understand a little more each time I read it or try to put it into practice. So, my last thanks go to Dr. Helen Schucman and Dr. William Thetford for bringing this book into our troubled world so that we can learn peace through forgiveness.

AUTHOR'S WEBSITES

www.thecourse.org.uk
www.healingthecause.org.uk

Forgiveness is the key to happiness.

Here is the answer to your search for peace. Here is the key to meaning in a world that seems to make no sense. Here is the way to safety in apparent dangers that appear to threaten you at every turn, and bring uncertainty to all your hopes of ever finding quietness and peace. Here are all questions answered; here the end of all uncertainty ensured at last.

From A Course in Miracles® – Lesson 121

INTRODUCTION

Peace of mind is a rare quality to find in this world. The strife we observe all around us mirrors the discord in our own minds. The path of forgiveness takes us back into ourselves where the source of all conflict begins. Forgiveness asks us to stop pointing our finger at the people and events in the world as the cause of our pain and turn instead to the unforgiven thoughts in our own minds. Here we can create change, which will lead to an ever-increasing sense of inner peace.

My inspiration for writing this book comes from *A Course in Miracles* (see appendix). In 1982, I visited the Findhorn Foundation in Scotland to take part in their Experience Week programme, where I discovered the *Course in Miracles* book displayed in the window of the Phoenix store at their Park site. I took it from the window, opened it at random, and read a paragraph. I cannot remember what I read, but I do remember the almost electric effect of the words upon me.

Each day, after lunch, I would remove the book from the window and read another paragraph. I did this for two weeks before I had to return home to London. Missing my midday read, I decided to purchase the book and study its teachings on forgiveness.

My studies coincided with a time when my interest in healing was developing, after discovering – by accident – that I could sometimes help people by the laying on of hands. In my healing work and research, I discovered that the mind exerts a very powerful effect on the body. Although people were helped by the laying on of hands, I found their problems would often return unless they forgave the thoughts in their mind which led to the dis-ease. In time, I developed a healing approach (see chapter Five) to help clients look at the unforgiveness in their minds and let it be healed by spirit.

In 1980, I felt guided to resign from my work as an electronics lecturer and explore a different path in life. Visiting the Findhorn Foundation and doing some healing work in London was part of this new adventure. Whilst visiting the Foundation in 1984 to take part in a workshop, my partner and I felt a strong spontaneous impulse to become members. We returned to London, sold our house, and moved to Findhorn. For three years I directed the healing department at the Foundation's Cluny Hill site. I went on to develop a two-week workshop entitled 'Healing the Cause', which I ran at the Foundation for some years. My background in teaching electronics in London was helpful, but I had to learn to be intuitively guided in my approach to teaching these workshops. This was a whole different arena, requiring a flexibility and openness never really required in my more technical role.

My study and practice of *A Course in Miracles* continued and deepened my knowledge of healing and the need to open myself to inner guidance. In my younger years, I had believed I could happily plan what I wanted from life and did not need anyone's help thank you! However, as my life progressed, it became clear that without a willing surrender to an inner guidance there was no chance I would discover the inner peace I sought.

My deepening interest in the Course and my experiences from the workshops led me to write a book (*Healing the Cause: A Path of Forgiveness*) and also resulted in me running even more workshops – both at the Findhorn Foundation and elsewhere. And of course, it has also now led to the writing of this book.

The path of forgiveness can be practised every day, for life presents us all with endless opportunities; it invites us to stop seeing the world as the source of our pain and encourages us to bring a non-judgemental awareness to the contents of our own mind – the only place where healing can occur. As we surrender our pain to the healing power of spirit, we gradually remove the veils we have created between our physical selves and our spiritual reality: a state of inner peace and joy that is not dependent on anything in the world.

In this book, I set out the steps required to take on this journey of forgiveness. I invite you to join me on this path to peace.

Chapter One

WHO DO WE FORGIVE?

Perhaps it will be helpful to remember that no one can be angry at a fact.
It is always an interpretation that gives rise to negative emotions,
regardless of their seeming justification by what **appears** as facts.

[A Course in Miracles® M-17.4[1]]

FORGIVENESS OF OURSELVES OR OTHERS?

Who needs to be forgiven? This is a fundamental question. Many of us believe we need to strive to forgive the wrongs that seem to have been done *to* us. We feel victimised by the seemingly unfair actions of others and believe our anger towards them is justified. But is it always the others who need to be forgiven, or could it maybe be ourselves? Do we have to remain victims or is there another way?

The personal tension created by holding grievances against another is unpleasant. We may feel we are in the right, but at great personal cost to our own peace of mind. To alleviate such tension we might choose to 'forgive' the other person; although in our opinion they have committed a wrong, we

[1] Please see Appendix 1 for an explanation of page and line references to *A Course in Miracles*.

decide to overlook it. We would, however, love to hear them apologise, proving *their* guilt and *our* innocence. But an apology may not be forthcoming; indeed the person with whom we hold our grievance may now have died.

We tell our friends we have forgiven our enemy; we are prepared to forget and get on with life. But have we really returned our mind to a state of peace, or is there lurking an ongoing disquiet about this episode? Do we carry on and forget the incident only to find that past pain is still there just waiting to be triggered by events similar to the one we have just 'forgiven'? Has our forgiveness worked? Has the willingness to put all this behind us and to overlook the sins of the other actually resolved anything?

Our cultural and religious upbringing generally decrees what is right and what is wrong behaviour. If someone acts towards us with 'wrong' behaviour, we are usually taught that our anger is justified; the other person *should* apologise and change his or her behaviour. If they conform to our expectations, we are then open to 'forgiving' them, but not otherwise.

The quotation at the start of this chapter reminds us that we never get angry over a fact: it's our interpretation of the fact that can give rise to anger. Forgiveness tells us we can always choose our reaction to any situation.

Consider the following story:

Imagine you are at a party with three friends. Let's call them John, Peter, and Mary. The topic of conversation gets around to a recent news story about the rise in obesity in the United Kingdom population and its effect on the National Health Service. It was clear from the article that diseases related to obesity were costing the NHS millions of pounds each year. The writer of the article felt it was unfair how the sector of the population that was not obese had to carry the financial penalty for those who are. One of his suggestions was that the obese should pay a contribution towards their treatment if they suffered from an obesity related illness.

John, who is somewhat overweight, feels this is an outrageous suggestion, clearly lacking in compassion for the plight of the obese. Peter, who keeps trim with regular workouts in the gym, thinks it an excellent suggestion; he is happy this issue has been raised in the national press, feeling it is high time something is done about it. This obvious clash of opinions soon provokes fierce discussion between the two men. Mary has stood by, quietly listening. Although being a bit overweight herself, she cannot muster any interest in this debate; her mind is more focused on the evening ahead.

In the above story, we can see how one event or stimulus – in this case the newspaper report – produced three entirely different responses. John was angry, Peter happy, and Mary indifferent. Each person chose his or her own response to the facts in the article.

No stimulus has any inherent power to create a certain response in all people. We ourselves always choose how we react in any given situation; there is nothing in this world that has the power to take our peace away. Yes, certain events can lead us to experience physical pain, but even in these events it is our personal choice whether to get upset about it or not.

I remember watching a dramatised documentary about a white fur trapper working within the Arctic Circle who became good friends with an Eskimo family. This Eskimo tribe had a particular custom, which was to share everything they possessed (including their wives) with close friends. One day the husband announced to the fur trapper that he would be very happy if he were to sleep with his wife. He added that it would also make his wife very happy; this was not a custom imposed upon the women, but something they happily agreed to. The fur trapper was shocked and declined their offer. His reaction upset the family deeply.

In one scene, the distressed wife asked the fur trapper why he had refused her: was it that she was ugly? Neither the husband nor the wife could understand why a close friend would not want to share their life. Contrast this response to what we might normally expect here in the West if a husband came home and found his wife in bed with his best friend! The typical response would be strong negative feelings such as anger, fear, outrage, and betrayal: an example of one stimulus causing opposite reactions. It follows that an event in itself cannot provoke an automatic response; it is always we who choose the response to any situation. This choice of response lies at the heart of forgiveness.

Let's make a start on our path of forgiveness with the following exercise:

Forgiveness Exercise:
For this exercise you will need a sheet of paper and a pen. Divide the sheet into two columns by drawing a line down the middle, and then put a line across the top for two headings, as shown in figure 1.1.

Example of Exercise

The qualities I like about .... are:	The qualities I dislike about ...... are:
gentleness	anger
sensitivity	when he drinks
caring	when he smokes
the way he dresses	laziness
good listener	jealousy

Fig 1.1

Think of someone you know very well, someone for whom you can list both likes and dislikes. This could be a parent, partner, lover, sister, brother, boss, or friend.
Now write the name of the person you have chosen as part of the following heading in the top left-hand box on your page:
    The qualities I like about …name… are:
In the top right hand box, write:
    The qualities I dislike about …name… are:
Now it's time to be honest: write at least four or five qualities you like about this person and four or five you dislike about them in the respective columns.
If you find you are struggling to get four or five likes and dislikes, add another name to the top boxes and simply continue adding to your lists. The more you write in your columns the more you may learn.
Spend a few minutes with this exercise and only when you are finished continue reading.

Please do not read any further until you have completed your lists, or it will lessen the impact of this exercise!

Now go back to the top of your lists, cross out the name/s on each side, and insert your own name instead. The lists now read as the qualities you like and dislike in yourself. Strange? But true! If you did not possess these qualities yourself, to some degree or another, you would not see them in others.

You may find it difficult to accept some of these qualities depending on the image you have of yourself. For instance, if you have low self-esteem you may find it impossible to believe that all these good qualities are within you. Maybe you find it embarrassing when people appreciate you and will deftly switch the topic of conversation if someone says something complimentary. If this sounds like you, you can be sure there is hidden guilt waiting to be forgiven, but don't despair, later on we will look at exercises that can be of help in this process

In the same way, the negative attributes you see in the other person must also be in yourself; otherwise, you would not be upset about them. Of course, it's possible to recognise character faults in another without having them yourself. However, in this exercise you need to list the things that really upset you about the other person. If something someone else does upsets you, this is the red flag that is showing you what is unforgiven in yourself.

For most of us, a recognition that something we dislike in someone else is actually something we also possess will be actively resisted, because in our minds we feel sure of two things:

- The *other* person has these particular negative attributes

and

- We want *them* to change these behaviours to ones we prefer.

That they have these negative attributes may or may not be true, but that is not important. What is important is that on some level you know that what you accuse them of is a reflection of something within you. Take jealousy as an example. Maybe your partner is jealous of your friends and this may mirror your jealousy of those who are wealthier than you. These are simply two different expressions of the same thing.

"There is nothing either good or bad, but thinking makes it so."
[William Shakespeare, "Hamlet" II.ii.259]

Typically, our conditioning tells us jealousy is wrong, it's bad, and we should not be jealous. Taking on this value judgement, we feel guilty and ashamed and may pretend we do not suffer from it. Or if we do admit we are jealous, then we'll pacify ourselves that it's only 'just a little'. But we know this is not really true, and don't want to face the fact. Consequently, when we see this fault in another we are uncomfortably reminded how – to some degree – we suffer from the same 'sin'.

When biologists want to understand the life and behaviour of some recently discovered animal species they need to do their work with non-judgemental awareness. Whilst watching the new species they may observe all manner of behaviour, including much that is brutal. For instance, perhaps the male of the species has to be prevented by the female from fighting or devouring their offspring. If biologists become upset and judgemental about the observed animal behaviour, they have lost the required detachment to actually record what is happening and may be tempted to analyse or explain behaviour from a human point of view.

In the same way, as we judge the facts of our nature we lose the ability to really see what is happening. We may become preoccupied with guilt at what we observe rather than working with acceptance and self-forgiveness. Instead, we quickly try to sweep it all under the carpet where we desperately hope it will be forgotten.

If we uncover the uncomfortable facts of our nature and resist labeling them as 'bad', we do have an opportunity to heal them. Fortunately, opportunities are presented to us daily as we come into contact with people and events that trigger what we have tried to lock away in our unconscious. The people we meet are our potential saviours, showing us – sometimes time and time again – what we have tried to bury in our minds.

Should you observe in another a particular negative behaviour that you either do not possess, or do possess but have forgiven in yourself, then you would not respond with upset, but rather with non-judgemental compassion for the other person. You would simply know their negative behaviour is caused by fear and they are doing their best to cope with something they find difficult; their behaviour would not be perceived as an attack upon you, but as a call for your help. They would be allowed to *be*, and you would be happy and willing to help if asked.

If you extend forgiveness to others, you automatically extend this forgiveness to yourself, too. What you give to others – whether in love or hate – you also give to yourself. Why? Because our actions reinforce the thoughts in our mind. If we act lovingly, we are reminding and reinforcing in ourselves that we are loving. Similarly, to attack another increases the hate and therefore guilt in our mind.

The behaviours in the dislike column may not apply to you in an obvious, direct way. Maybe you listed anger, yet you never get angry with the person whose name you started out with. But what if you do carry suppressed anger that makes you feel ashamed, and this is what you are being reminded of? Rather than directly expressing your anger back to them, you may withdraw and act remote around this person.

Perhaps you dislike a person drinking alcohol because you virtually never drink. Try to look at your thoughts and feelings when you are in the company of this person. Why *does* it bother you so that they drink? Are they maybe drinking to escape from the pain in their life? Do you also seek to escape from the pain in your life but use other means, perhaps overeating, or excessive viewing of TV or browsing of the Internet?

Take a few minutes to look again at your 'negative' column on the list you made earlier.

Do you feel there is some truth in what it says about you? Our egos hate this type of exposure! We prefer to deny what is in our subconscious and project it out onto the world instead. Rather than look at ourselves, we blame everyone else: our mother, father, partner, employer, the government, this dictator, that religion, and so on. To start the process of forgiveness we need to take responsibility for what is in our own minds, and in the next chapter we will explore more fully our ego's story of denial and projection.

∞∞∞

In every situation where we lose our peace, we have found a reflection of what is unhealed, what we have not forgiven ourselves for. We all walk around in a hall of mirrors, the world constantly reflecting back what is in our minds. When we are upset the world becomes a messenger, drawing our attention to what we have tried to ignore or even failed to recognise. Instead of killing the messenger, we now have an opportunity to work with forgiveness – of ourselves.

You may agree with some or all of what you've read so far, but may have serious reservations about whether this applies to events on the world stage such as war and genocide, murder and rape. How can we forgive such atrocities? This is an important question and will be explored more fully in the next chapter.

I will end this introduction with a letter I received from a friend; it illustrates well the fact that we don't have to change other people to feel at peace around them:

> I built up a strong hate relationship with the man who owns the town's hardware store. I often had to go in there and found him the rudest, most overbearing rip-off merchant I'd ever met. After eight months or so, I vowed never to go there again, though it meant a lot of trouble for me. I also decided to put anyone else off going there.
>
> One day, I urgently needed photocopying done of some children's sanctuary songs for a group the next day. Songs like 'The more we are together', 'You are beautiful', etc. Of course, he has the only photocopier in town so I went in hoping to slip down to his photocopy room and do it myself but, instead, he came with me and proceeded to do the photocopying. As he did, he got interested in the songs and asked me how they went.
>
> I very reluctantly began to sing these very spiritual songs. He joined in, in a gorgeous baritone, rich and full. I think we sang our way through every

song! This transformed everything. I didn't intend to 'forgive', we just joined, and it happened. His voice was so beautiful that I was transfixed and the ridiculousness of the situation appealed to my nature.

I adore the man now and see so many sides of him that were invisible before. Although I still end up buying three things I don't need whenever I go into his shop, I can admire the fact that he is the only thriving business in the village.

I feel so much joy when I remember this incident. I think it should be on a film. Importantly to me, he didn't change at all; he didn't have to. I wish I could do this as easily with all the other people who annoy me!

Krissy, New Zealand

SUMMARY

- Facts are neutral
- No event in the world produces the same response in everyone
- We always choose our reactions to situations
- What upsets us about others reflects what is unforgiven in ourselves

Chapter Two

THE EGO'S WORLD

Perception is a mirror, not a fact. And what I look on is my state of mind,
reflected outward [...] Everything you perceive is a witness
to the thought system you want to be true.

[*A Course in Miracles. W-pII.304.1:3-4; T-II.V.18:3*]

In this chapter, we will look more closely at some of the issues that were raised
in the previous one. In particular, we will discuss guilt, denial, and projection,
which are attributes of the ego. I am using the term ego to describe that part
of our self that feels separated, lonely and isolated and in need of constant
defence in a world perceived as threatening.

It is the ego that feels guilty, inadequate, fearful, sure that anger will get it
what it wants; it feels persecuted by the world and justified in attacking back.
Ego cannot conceive of another way of acting in the world: kill or be killed
is its motto. Never does it realise the problem is in its own mind, believing
happiness will come if it can just change the world to suit its needs. However,
there is another part of our mind that thinks the opposite to the ego and we
can decide to listen to this instead. That will be the focus of chapter four, but
first we need to understand some of the mechanisms of the ego.

Sigmund Freud first introduced the concept of defence mechanisms;

techniques we develop to defend against anxiety and to maintain self-esteem. Freud identified a number of these mechanisms, including denial and projection.

When in denial, we refuse to recognise a threatening situation or thought. We can even bring into play another defence mechanism, that of rationalisation, where we attempt to excuse or explain our behaviour in a rational manner. For example, a person may refuse to acknowledge the effect of excessive alcohol intake by maintaining that wine is good for the health.

Projection is an involuntary process motivated by impulses and emotions wherein a person imposes a subjective feeling or a thought onto others. For example, a seemingly jealous husband may accuse his wife of being unfaithful, while in reality it is he who secretly wants to embark upon an affair.

GUILT AND DENIAL

> One does not become enlightened by imagining figures of light,
> but by making the darkness conscious.
>
> *[C.G. Jung]*

Guilt is the sum total of all the negative feelings and thoughts we have about ourselves: our lack of self-worth, feelings of inadequacy, inferiority complexes, shame, and inherent unworthiness. However, we are only aware of a small percentage of this guilt; it is like an iceberg, most of it lurking beneath the surface of our conscious mind. But we do still suffer from its presence, even though most of it is suppressed or denied.

Unconscious guilt is easily triggered by events in the world, and whenever it resurfaces we feel very uncomfortable and desire to get rid of the feeling as soon as possible. We may turn to the event that triggered the unconscious guilt and blame that as the source of our unease. If we are not sufficiently aware to catch what we are doing, we easily get lost in the guilt/attack cycle (Figure 2.1.):

The Guilt/Attack Cycle

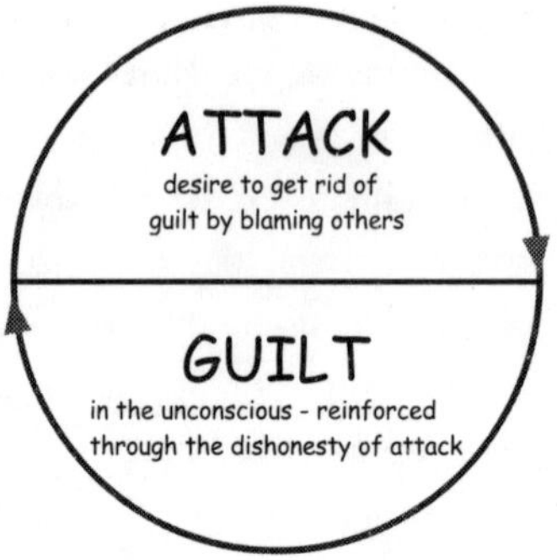

ATTACK
desire to get rid of
guilt by blaming others

GUILT
in the unconscious - reinforced
through the dishonesty of attack

Fig. 2.1

Stage 1   An event triggers our unconscious guilt. For example, someone tells us we are lazy. Although we are aware that in most parts of life we are actually hard working, we are also conscious that in some areas we don't try hard enough. The guilt around this issue is now triggered.

Stage 2   The shame we feel rises into our conscious mind. We instantly become very uncomfortable with this feeling, and our desire is to get rid of it as fast as possible.

Stage 3   Our ego immediately informs us there's nothing wrong with us (denial), but there is certainly something wrong with the accuser (projection); it tells us we have been unfairly treated and victimised, and our resultant anger is justified. It counsels us to attack the other person so we can make them feel guilty, in the hope that their resultant guilt will make them change their behaviour into something acceptable to us. For example, we may receive an apology and this will reinforce our idea that there is nothing wrong with us, for the apology now declares the other person is at fault. If no apology is forthcoming, our ego will tell us to become even angrier in the hope of attaining our desired goal.

Stage 4   Making another person responsible for the guilt in our minds is a dishonest act. It does not matter whether the person apologises or not, for we know at some level that our attack upon them is unjustified. All this serves to increase our level of guilt, which, once again, we try and get rid of by attacking the other. This is the vicious cycle of guilt and attack that can only be broken through forgiveness of ourselves.

If only we could see it! The person we have chosen to attack is actually doing us a favour; we are being shown our unconscious guilt, and if we so choose, we could now try to heal it. This is the great value of all relationships: they bring unconscious guilt to the surface. We then have the choice of following our ego's advice, which is to attack, or to follow that wiser part of our mind, which counsels forgiveness of ourselves.

PROJECTION

Our ego is always looking for someone or something to blame. It doesn't matter who the enemy is, sometimes we may even choose an inanimate object. Do you know the famous sketch from Fawlty Towers, where John Cleese beats his car with a tree branch because it won't start? He is blaming his car for his guilt over being late, and that really isn't so very far-fetched, people *do* things like that. A more common example might be the door that refuses to stay shut. You repeatedly try to close it with increasing force until eventually losing your temper and banging it so hard it may never open again, shouting, "That will show you who's boss!" Now was it really the door that made you so cross? If we are capable of doing that to an innocent door, imagine what we can project onto people.

The ego requires a 'scapegoat' – an interesting term which warrants some explanation. When the Israelites wandered the desert, each year the high priest would gather the tribe and arrange for a goat to be placed before him. Laying his hands upon the head of the goat, he would announce that he was taking all the sins of the people before him and transferring them into the goat. The goat would then be driven out of the camp taking – the tribe believed – all their sins with it.

Thousands of years later and this practice continues daily, though we're no longer choosing goats to carry away our guilt. Instead, we may choose a particular race of people, for example black people, Jewish people, or gypsies. Let me explain a little further: During the time when India was a colony of Great Britain, the British were an obvious target for hatred, and this hatred helped to unify the Hindus and Muslims in a common cause. However, once the British left so did a convenient scapegoat. The ego had to find a new enemy and the Hindus and Muslims quickly began to attack each other instead. This goes on worldwide and the desire for these scapegoats will never end until we accept the responsibility for healing the guilt in our own minds.

To help deepen our understanding of projection lets take a look at Fig 2.2. Do you see the face of a young or an old woman? If you see the face of an old woman, you might be wondering what I am talking about – or vice versa.

Fig 2.2

So, which is the correct answer? They both are!

- If you can only see the old face try looking at the right eye again, but now see it as the right ear of a young woman who is facing right. The nose of the old woman now becomes the cheek of the young woman.

- If you can only see the face of the young woman try looking again at her ear, but now see it as the right eye of the old woman. The cheek of the young woman now becomes the large nose of the old woman.

What has the mind been doing here? Data from the drawing enters the eye and forms an inverted two-dimensional image on the back of the eye, the retina. This is translated into electrochemical pulses that are sent by the optic nerve to the rear of the brain. The brain searches its data bank of images, decides on the most appropriate match, and projects that onto the picture. In other words, we see what we want to see and not necessarily what's there.

Fig 2.3

Now take a look at Fig 2.3. Most people will see a white triangle. However, I think we would all agree that no such triangle actually exists, although our minds have projected one onto the diagram. Such is the power of projection!

If we are capable of seeing what's not there in the case of a simple, objective drawing, imagine our ability to get it wrong in the case of our psychological projections onto others – or other 'things' (remember the ill-fitting door?). Just as in the case of the above visual projections, our psychological projections also insist they are true and not open to question.

When we discuss the first stage of forgiveness in Chapter Four we will see how important it is to take back into our own mind the negative things we have projected onto others. This does not mean we can't observe accurately the behaviour of others – such as the sadistic behaviour of a cruel dictator – but if the behaviour of this dictator is causing us to feel anger then there is a denied and therefore unforgiven dictator in our own mind. This is what taking back the projection means.

Of course you may never do anything as bad as the cruel dictator, but there are other ways in which we can be dictatorial. Using our power to take what we want is dictatorial behaviour. We may do this subtly by manipulation of another, or by using our greater physical strength over others – our children perhaps.

As long as we project the problem outside our minds and onto the world there is no chance of healing ourselves. It is only when we see it within ourselves that the healing can begin.

A story I heard about a participant in a workshop by Dr. Kenneth Wapnick makes a good illustration of this point:

During the workshop the topic of hating in another what you have denied in yourself had been raised. A large man stood up and protested at this teaching. He told the class that some months before he had witnessed a young girl being deliberately pushed in front of an oncoming underground train. The incident had remained with him for months and he felt distressed and very angry at what he had seen. "Surely," he exclaimed, "you are not telling me I am capable of that behaviour. I refuse to believe it!" He sat down and the workshop continued.

Towards the end of the workshop he stood up again and shared the following insight: He told the class that kids liked to play with him, and he thought his bulk was part of the reason for this. In fact, he was always asked at Christmas time to dress up as Father Christmas and distribute presents to the children. He hated the job but could not bring himself to refuse. The kids would get up on his lap, play with his beard and generally torment him. Although he suppressed his feelings, he admitted he wanted to fling these kids off him – just as the man he saw at the underground had flung a young child onto the rail tracks. He now understood why that scene had haunted him for so long. In seeing this, he had withdrawn his projection from the killer and brought it back to his own mind where the process of forgiveness could begin.

Some other examples of projection are shown in Fig 2.4. In all cases, the real problem of unconscious guilt in the mind is projected out onto the world, from where it is then believed to originate.

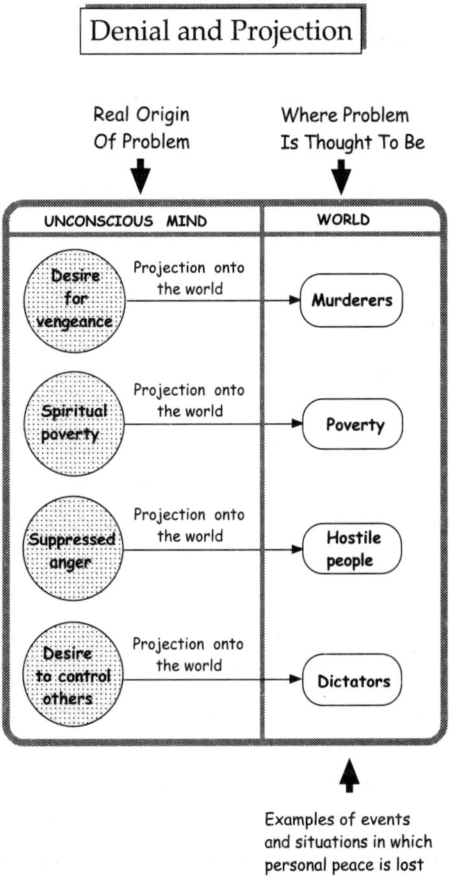

Denial and Projection

Real Origin Of Problem	Where Problem Is Thought To Be

UNCONSCIOUS MIND		WORLD
Desire for vengeance	Projection onto the world	Murderers
Spiritual poverty	Projection onto the world	Poverty
Suppressed anger	Projection onto the world	Hostile people
Desire to control others	Projection onto the world	Dictators

Fig 2.4

Examples of events and situations in which personal peace is lost

For example, if we get *really* upset about murderers and think they deserve the very strongest punishment, we are actually experiencing the effects of our denied desire for vengeance. We feel a strong desire to get even with those who we perceive as having treated us unfairly but would feel very ashamed to realise that we too are capable of murder. We only need to look at what happens to 'ordinary' people in times of war, where often the slightest excuse is all that is needed to kill another.

This is a good time to go back to the list you made during the exercise in chapter one. If you had trouble seeing the truth about yourself in the negative projections you wrote down, perhaps it will seem clearer now. I realise what a dreadful exercise that was for your ego, as it is the complete opposite of what we are normally taught. We live in a blame culture.

Yes, forgiveness is very hard to do for it turns our world upside down. How can we carry on being victims with our justified anger when we start to realise we always choose our response to situations? In Chapter Three we will look more deeply at why it's so hard to forgive.

A STORY OF FORGIVENESS

When the war in Europe ended in May 1945, the 123rd Evac unit entered Germany with the occupying troops. I was part of a group assigned to a concentration camp near Wuppertal, charged with getting medical help to the newly liberated prisoners, many of them Jews from Holland, France, and eastern Europe. This was the most shattering experience I had yet had; I had been exposed many times by then to sudden death and injury, but to see the effects of slow starvation, to walk through those barracks where thousands of men had died a little bit at a time over a period of years, was a new kind of horror. For many it was an irreversible process: we lost scores each day in spite of all the medicine and food we could rush to them.

Now I needed my new insight indeed. When the ugliness became too great to handle I did what I had learned to do. I went from one end to the other of that barbed wire enclosure looking into men's faces until I saw looking back at me the face of Christ.

And that's how I came to know Wild Bill Cody. That wasn't his real name. His real name was seven unpronounceable syllables in Polish, but he had a long drooping handlebar mustache like pictures of the old western hero, so the American soldiers called him Wild Bill. He was one of the inmates of the concentration camp, but obviously he hadn't been there long: his posture was erect, his eyes bright, his energy indefatigable. Since he was fluent in English, French, German and Russian, as well as Polish, he became a kind of unofficial camp translator.

We came to him with all sorts of problems; the paper work alone was staggering in attempting to relocate people whose families, even whole hometowns, might have disappeared. But though Wild Bill worked fifteen and sixteen hours a day, he showed no signs of weariness. While the rest of us were drooping with fatigue, he seemed to gain strength. "We have time for this old fellow," he'd say. "He's been waiting to see us all day." His compassion for his fellow prisoners glowed on his face, and it was to this glow that I came when my own spirits were low.

So I was astonished to learn when Wild Bill's own papers came before us one day, that he had been in Wuppertal since 1939! For six years he had lived on the same starvation diet, slept in the same airless and disease-ridden barracks as everyone else, but without the least physical or mental deterioration.

Perhaps even more amazing, every group in the camp looked on him as a friend. He was the one to whom quarrels between inmates were brought for arbitration. Only after I'd been at Wuppertal a number of weeks did I realize what a rarity this was in a compound where the different nationalities of prisoners hated each other almost as much as they did the Germans.

As for Germans, feeling against them ran so high that in some of the camps liberated earlier, former prisoners had seized guns, run into the nearest village and simply shot the first Germans they saw. Part of our instructions were to prevent this kind of thing and again Wild Bill was our greatest asset, reasoning with the different groups, counseling forgiveness.

"It's not easy for some of them to forgive," I commented to him one day as we sat over mugs of tea in the processing center. So many of them have lost members of their families"

Wild Bill leaned back in the upright chair and sipped at his drink. "We lived in the Jewish section of Warsaw," he began slowly, the first words I had heard him speak about himself, "my wife, our two daughters, and our three little boys. When the Germans reached our street they lined everyone against a wall and opened up with machine guns. I begged to be allowed to die with my family, but because I spoke German they put me in a work group."

He paused, perhaps seeing again his wife and five children. "I had to decide right then," he continued, "whether to let myself hate the soldiers who had done this. It was an easy decision, really. I was a lawyer. In my practice I had seen too often what hate could do to people's minds and bodies. Hate had just killed the six people who mattered most to me in the world. I decided then that I would spend the rest of my life – whether it was a few days or many years – loving every person I came in contact with

> *[From Return from Tomorrow by George Ritchie, M.D.*
> *© 1978 published by Fleming H. Revell, a division of*
> *Baker Book House Company.]*

One of the hallmarks of the ego is that it always takes sides: there are always 'goodies' and 'baddies'. Wild Bill did not take sides. It mattered not to him whether the people he helped were so-called 'victims' or 'persecutors'; they were both unhappy and consciously or unconsciously calling for love, which he then gave. It is clear from the above story that Wild Bill did not see himself in either category either and this enabled him to retain his peace under the most demanding of circumstances. It also allowed him to access a source of energy and reserve within himself that allowed him to survive the camps. So much so that he had more energy than the well fed doctors who had come to help the inmates of the camp!

Earlier, I talked about how all things that happen are neutral and we ourselves decide how to react. In the case of Wild Bill, we see how an event judged as horrific by the world became the means by which a saint was born on earth. Seeing the world as neutral does not, of course, condone the affliction of pain and death on others, but reminds us that we can still choose how we respond to situations we find ourselves in.

Wild Bill was an exceptional man who, in exceptional circumstances, chose forgiveness as his path.

FORGIVENESS AND WORLD EVENTS

Projection makes perception.
The world you see is what you gave it, nothing more than that.
But though it is no more than that, it is not less.
Therefore to you it is important. It is the witness to your state of mind,
the outside picture of an inward condition.
As a man thinketh, so does he perceive. Therefore, seek not to change the
world, but choose to change your mind about the world.

[A Course in Miracles T-21.1.1:1-7]

A question often raised is: "How is it possible to forgive the horrendous events we have witnessed on the world stage?" Forgiveness of our personal flaws is difficult, but possible, but when we witness events such as the deliberate extermination of thirteen million people by the Nazis should we even consider forgiveness at all? Are some events unforgivable?

It took the co-operation of thousands of Germans to murder such a large number of people. When leading Nazis were questioned at the Nuremberg trials about why they permitted this atrocity the responses: "I was only following orders," or "doing my duty," or "I was just a cog in the wheel" were heard over and over again.

When Adolf Eichmann stood trial in Jerusalem for his part in the Holocaust the prosecution attempted to depict him as a sadistic monster. In reply, he stated he was just a bureaucrat with a desk job he had been entrusted to carry out efficiently. Even he was sickened when he toured concentration camps. Can we believe such excuses?

Is it conceivable that ordinary citizens can inflict pain and even death upon innocent people under the pretence of following orders? Is there a hidden Eichmann in each of us? How far are we willing to go in our obedience to authority? Could these horrors be repeated again? If we all have a hidden Nazi in our own minds and we do not discover and forgive it, I believe – under certain circumstances – that ordinary people could and would again perform these horrendous immoral acts against millions of innocent people.

In the USA in the early 1960s Stanley Milgram carried out an experiment at Yale University[2] on obedience to authority. I would like to describe certain aspects of this experiment in some detail as they shed considerable light on the above questions.

Milgram was interested in seeing how far a voluntary participant would comply with increasingly callous instructions before refusing to carry out any further actions. He was careful to include a wide cross-section of male volunteers, who were paid by the hour and were free to leave whenever they wished.

In one experiment, two volunteers were involved with research into the effects of punishment on learning. The experimenter was a 31-year old man who, dressed in a grey technician's coat, projected an impassive manner and appeared stern throughout the experiment. The volunteers drew lots to decide who was to be the 'teacher' and who the 'learner'. Once decided, the teacher watched the learner be strapped into a chair, with an electrode attached to his wrist. The learner was told this was a learning test and whenever he made a mistake, he would receive an electric shock from the teacher. These shocks were to increase in intensity with each mistake. The experimenter's job was to supervise the experiment and ensure the teacher correctly followed procedure.

The teacher was taken to an adjacent room, from where he could not see the learner. There he sat before an impressive electric shock generator with a

---

[2] *Obedience to Authority* by Stanley Milgram. Pinter and Martin Ltd, 1997.

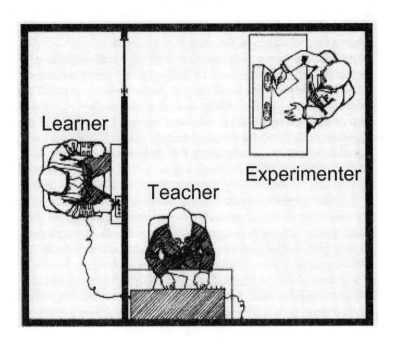

panel of 30 switches, ranging – in 15 volt intervals – from 15 volts though to 450 volts. Labels reading Slight Shock, Moderate Shock, Strong Shock and Danger: Severe Shock were placed adjacent to groups of switches. There were also two switches marked XXX. When a switch was depressed a bright red light shone, a buzzer sounded and the pointer on a voltage meter swung to the right.

A sample shock of 45 volts (slight shock) was given to the wrist of each teacher prior to starting the experiment, so he could feel the effect and appreciate the pain that could be inflicted at higher voltages.

The teacher began to ask questions and if the response was incorrect he would administer an electric shock to the learner. The first shock was 15 volts and they increased in level by 15 volts each time thereafter.

Now here comes the twist. The teacher was a genuine volunteer, but unknown to him the learner was an actor, who never actually received a shock at all. Most participants found the learner mild-mannered and likeable. The actor was instructed to give enough wrong answers to guarantee him eventually receiving the maximum shock (assuming the teacher did as he was told!). The idea was to determine how far the teacher was willing to go in following the orders of the experimenter.

The male actor (learner) was told to give auditory feedback at certain voltages. These included a grunt at 75 volts, verbally complaining at 120 volts, demanding to be released at 150 volts, shouting that he couldn't stand the pain at 180 volts, about his heart condition at 195 volts and various cries of pain leading to an agonised scream at 285 volts. After 330 volts he was to say nothing. Instead there was an ominous silence.

As the experiment progressed the severity of the shocks started to cause some apparent discomfort in the learner. At this point the teacher started to ask the experimenter if he should continue administering higher voltages. The experimenter had a set of standard responses beginning with, "Please go on". If this did not bring the teacher into line he would move onto the next 'prod': "The experiment requires you to continue". And if that was unsuccessful he would say, "It is absolutely essential that you go on," and finally, "You have no other choice, you must go on".

If the teacher expressed concern about possible permanent physical injury the experimenter would reply with: "Although the shocks may be painful, there is no permanent tissue damage, so please go on". If the teacher mentioned that the learner wanted to stop, the experimenter would say, "Whether the learner likes it or not, you must go on until he has learned all the word pairs correctly. So please go on." If the learner made no reply, which would occur at voltages above 330 volts, the teacher was told no reply was an incorrect reply, so the next highest shock must be administered.

What would you do if you drew the lot to be the teacher? How far would you be willing to comply with the orders of the experimenter? Would you be capable of administering apparently painful and dangerous electric shocks, rationalising that you were only following orders? Or are only sadistic monsters capable of doing such things?

To test what people might expect of themselves under such circumstances,

Milgram lectured audiences on the experiment and then asked them to predict their behaviour. Predictions were made by psychiatrists, college students, and middle-class adults. All 110 respondents said they would at some point break off the experiment to prevent further suffering. They were then asked to predict how other people would perform and the different groups responded in a very similar fashion, predicting that only a pathological fringe would go to the end and administer the highest XXX shock. The psychiatrists predicted that most subjects would not exceed the 150 volt level and only one subject in a thousand would administer the highest shock. In other words, they expected people to be merciful and unwilling to administer painful shocks.

So what actually happened?

The results were a complete surprise for Milgram and his team. The percentage of obedient male subjects who went all the way and delivered the maximum shock was 62.5 percent. Repeating the experiment with female volunteers produced a result of 65 percent administering the maximum shock.

Did these findings indicate that over half the people of the USA were sadists? The results showed that there were 600 times as many volunteers ready to give the full shock than the psychiatrists predicted.

Milgram devised another experiment almost identical to the one described, the difference being that this time the teacher could choose which level of shock to apply for wrong answer; the majority chose only slight or moderate levels of shock, with only one of the 40 volunteers administering the maximum level. Clearly, the great majority of volunteers were not motivated to harm the learner and many experienced considerable discomfort when told to apply increasing shock levels.

In another experiment, the teacher did not have to press the switches personally but had to tell another volunteer (an actor) to press them instead. The second 'volunteer' would always comply with the teacher's instructions. The percentage of obedient teachers now rose to 92.5 per cent. Their willingness to inflict pain increased dramatically as long as they were giving the order and not doing it themselves.

What became abundantly clear to Milgram was that the majority of us will conform to the instructions of someone we perceive as an authority, even if it means administering extreme pain and death to another.

> "The disappearance of a sense of responsibility is the most
> far-reaching consequence of submission to authority."
> *[Stanley Milgram]*

When the obedient volunteers were questioned after the experiment about their responses it was common to hear replies similar to those heard at the Nuremberg trials, namely, "I was only doing what I was told to do. I wanted to carry out the instructions properly".

Milgram noted that many subjects harshly devalued the learner. Comments such as, "He was so stupid and stubborn he deserved to get shocked,"[3] were common. These obvious rationalisations helped the participants to accept their own inhuman behaviour towards the victim. In one interview, a man who had administered the maximum shock was happy about his performance and told his wife he had done a good job. "Suppose the man was dead?" she asked. He replied, "So he's dead. I did my job!"[4].

When you consider the scale and the long period of time with which Nazi propaganda was directed against the Jews it becomes easier to see how many ordinary citizens can become so compliant with monstrous policies put out by people in authority. History continues to repeat itself.

I think Milgram's experiments point to one of the important factors that contribute to the perpetuation of atrocities: the majority of people are all too ready to give up their moral responsibilities to someone they perceive as an authority. We may think we are moral and upstanding citizens who would not inflict callous treatment on another, but when tested we can fail miserably. We don't know ourselves sufficiently well; buried under a barrier of denial are things most of us would rather not face. Honestly looking at ourselves is unpleasant, distressing, and stressful work; not something we can easily bring ourselves to do. But we need to unearth these parts of ourselves with

---

[3] *Ibid.* Page 27.

[4] *Ibid.* Page 106.

the help of the mirror of everyday experience. In this daily classroom of life we can see how readily most of us give up our moral responsibility to those in authority. It is important that when we observe this behaviour in ourselves we do not judge it, because by honestly facing what we find, accepting it and asking within for help we will eventually let it go. This is how we forgive and heal ourselves.

Unless we can admit we may carry an 'Eichmann' hidden inside our minds history is doomed to repeat itself.

My late wife Salice had an experience in February 1992 – around the time of the first Gulf War – that illustrated the common belief that we think our problems are out in the world, not within our minds. Salice was meditating and reflecting on Saddam Hussein and on the situation in Iraq and Kuwait. She felt helpless, there were so many terrible things happening out there, and she wanted to do something to help.

"What on earth can I do?" she asked.

A voice in her mind responded with a question: "How do you see Saddam Hussein?"

"As cruel, controlling, attacking and angry!"

"And do you have any of these traits?"

Salice thought deeply before admitting that she did indeed manifest these traits at times.

"Then this is what you can do: fix these things in yourself. That is the greatest gift you can give the Gulf War."

She was then shown a picture of Saddam Hussein standing on top of a mountain with all the people of the world gathered around its base. Saddam Hussein was holding a large mirror and the light was glinting on it. He was saying, "Look at me. You can't see these qualities inside yourselves so I am being a mirror for you and I have to exaggerate them in order for you to see them." Salice said she knew in that moment that whilst she or anyone else has any negative quality, it is always eventually projected onto something or someone else.[5]

---

[5] Reprinted from *Healing the Cause – A Path of Forgiveness*, Michael Dawson. Findhorn Press. 1994

"It may be that we are puppets – puppets controlled
by the strings of society. But at least we are puppets with perception,
with awareness. And perhaps our awareness is the first step
to our liberation."

[Stanley Milgram, 1974]

fORGIVENESS AND SICKNESS

Sickness takes many forms, and so does unforgiveness.
The forms of one but reproduce the forms of the other, for they are the
same illusion. So closely is one translated into the other, that a careful study
of the form a sickness takes will point quite clearly to the form
of unforgiveness that it represents. Yet seeing this will not effect a cure.
That is achieved by only one recognition; that only forgiveness heals an
unforgiveness, and only an unforgiveness can possibly
give rise to sickness of any kind.

*[Psychotherapy: Purpose, Process and Practice
P-2.VI.5 Supplement to* A Course in Miracles*]*

The above quotation makes a powerful statement: that the origin of sickness is
in the mind and not the body. Grievances held in the mind can become mirrored in the body as particular ailments – as dis-ease. Even our language gives
us pointers: "Get off my back", "You are a pain in the neck", "You make me
sick", and so on. Thankfully, just as a lack of forgiveness can result in physical
disease, forgiveness can heal the same.

Case Study – Sue[6]

Sue was a client of mine. Her work as a massage therapist was becoming
difficult because of a pain in her right arm and she was concerned whether
she could continue with her work. During our session, Sue began to see a
shadowy picture and experience feelings of fear. She had difficulty understanding what the picture was but felt it might be a face, as it appeared to

---

[6] Names have been changed in all histories.

have a nose. However, the nose was not really the right shape. I encouraged her to just let the picture be and to stay with the feeling of fear. Suddenly, the picture became clear: It was not a face at all; it was male genitals. The 'nose' was a penis.

In the scene that unfolded, she was a young girl being forced to masturbate her uncle using her right hand. Despite pain in her arm, the uncle would not let her stop until he was satisfied. On seeing this, Sue experienced a strong sensation of anger. After venting her anger, the remainder of the session was concerned with whether she was ready to let this feeling go. She was partially successful and her feedback, a few days later, was that her arm was much improved.

∞∞∞

A dramatic illustration of the mind-body link is provided in the case of people with multiple personalities, where the physiological state of their bodies can change when different personalities take control. This can result in particular ailments – even allergies – appearing or disappearing when a different personality/person comes to the front. And this can lead to all manner of problems for the medical profession, as well as the individual requiring treatment.

> Differences in allergic reactions among members of the 'family' have resulted in cases of allergies completely fading away as another personality takes control of the body. By changing the personality some multiples who are drunk can instantly become sober. If a child personality takes over a sedated adult personality the adult dosage may be too much for the child and result in an overdose.
>
> *[From The Holographic Universe, M. Talbot, HarperCollins]*

Here's one definition of this very complex disorder:

> Dissociative Identity Disorder (formerly known as Multiple Personality Disorder) is the presence of two or more distinct identities or personality states recurrently taking control of the person's behaviour. This leads to an

inability to recall important personal information that is too extensive to be explained by ordinary forgetfulness. It is commonly thought to be a survival tactic developed by highly traumatised children to protect themselves from the memory and effects of trauma and abuse. These children dissociate or block trauma from their conscious memories and place it in compartments or separate personalities within their self.

[Diagnostic Statistics Manual – version IV]

Other people seem to have developed 'natural multiples' without being abused and/or traumatised. They often refer to themselves as 'multiples' or 'plurals' in which many people share one mind, taking turns managing the body.

"It has all the benefits and drawbacks that you would find in any other group of people. It is not automatically a disorder [...] Individuals in the group may be of any age, religion, orientation, race, or gender – just like any other random group of people."

[a plural] [7]

As different people/personalities take control of the body, they bring with them different mindsets. The body acts like a puppet with the mind pulling the strings. A different mindset can bring about a physiological change.

There has been much research into multiple personalities. Psychologist, Dr. Nancy Perry, observed, "The different personalities have different brain waves, different blood pressure, vital signs, different allergies, different blood reactions; some of them are left-handed and some of them are right-handed."[8]

Multiple personalities can prove problematic for criminal investigators and can be baffling for experts, as N Humphrey and D.C.Dennett found: "Preliminary evidence, for example, of changes in handedness, voice-patterns, evoked-response brain-activity, and cerebral blood flow. When samples of

[7] "What is Multiplicity" www.kitsune.cx/blackbirds/layman/resource.html
[8] From an interview with Dr. Nancy Perry, a psychologist who works with multiples. Dave Baum Show. WBBM News Radio 78. June 27, 1990 www.astraeasweb.net/plural/newsline.html

the different handwritings of a multiple are mixed with samples by different hands, police handwriting experts have been unable to identify them."[9]

All this evidence forces us to look more closely at the mind-body link. It also gives a further incentive to practise forgiveness. Holding onto our un-forgiveness not only causes us to lose our sense of emotional and mental well being, but contributes to physical ill health as well.

∞∞∞

A friend once recounted a story of her struggle to finish with a job that was exhausting her. Jean helped run a centre for refugees; the work involved long hours and was emotionally demanding. Initially Jean was fuelled by enthu-siasm but had now reached a stage where she wanted to leave. The problem she faced was that the rest of her colleagues were already overworked and her leaving would only add to their problems. Every time Jean intended to tell someone she wanted to leave she would be overcome with guilt and continue working instead.

One day, whilst shopping in town, Jean was overcome with the feeling that she was in an impossible situation and she inwardly cried out: "I must stop working now!" On her way from one shop to another a car mounted the pavement and ran over her foot. Jean spent the next few weeks resting at home and put in her notice, as she was no longer able to work. This painful invocation demonstrates the power of our minds – even if we are not aware of it. Forgiving her guilt about leaving people in need would have allowed her to leave her work in peace. In retrospect, Jean knew there had been a more grace-ful option of forgiveness but she was unable to take it, at least this time.

If we are afraid of taking the next step in life, we may resort to sickness or an accident as a defence against the truth. Perhaps a long-term relationship is coming to an end and one of the partners fears the necessary separation. This partner may choose sickness in the hope that the other person will stay and look after him or her. Fear is often associated with change and sickness

---

[9] From *Speaking for Ourselves*, N Humphrey and D.C.Dennett. Raritan: A Quarterly Review, IX, 68-98, Summer 1989. Reprinted (with footnotes), www.astraeasweb.net/plural/speaking.html

can be seen as a good defence, distracting us from what is really happening and moving the focus onto the body. In this way, we need no longer confront the real issue but let the body take centre stage instead.

Sickness is a decision. It is not a thing that happens to you, quite unsought, which makes you weak and brings you suffering. It is a choice you make, a plan you lay, when for an instant truth arises in your own deluded mind, and all your world appears to totter and prepare to fall. Now you are sick, that truth may go away and threaten your establishments no more.

[A Course in Miracles W-pI.136.71-4]

If instead we choose the path of forgiveness, we will become non-judgementally aware of what is really happening in our lives, realising change is needed and how it would serve us. Then we can turn to our inner guide and ask for help to move forward and take the next step in our growth. Choosing sickness or an accident only painfully delays the day when forgiveness will finally be chosen.

Accepting that the source of our problems – both physical and psychological – is within our own mind and not in the world allows healing to occur. If the cause of our problems is seen in the 'outside' world, healing must wait. We can still have success in treating the effects of our sickness and, of course, medicine may help us dampen down the symptoms. However, as long as the underlying grievance or fear remains unforgiven, the dis-ease will manifest in a similar or related form.

The realisation of the mind-body link reveals to us that healing is now possible and it is our responsibility to start this journey.

INTRODUCTION TO THE LADDER OF FORGIVENESS

Up to this point we have been exploring the question of who needs to be forgiven and we have realised that forgiveness is always of ourselves and not of another. If it is clearly seen that it is our choice when we give away our peace in exchange for a grievance, we can start to climb the ladder of forgiveness.

The Ladder of Forgiveness

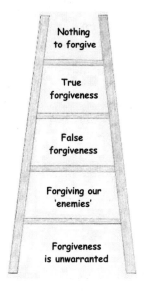

Nothing
to forgive

True
forgiveness

False
forgiveness

Forgiving our
'enemies'

Forgiveness
is unwarranted

Fig 2.5

In the next two chapters, we will explore the steps on this ladder. My inspiration for these chapters comes from *The Song of Prayer* – a supplement to *A Course in Miracles*.

At the bottom of the ladder, even before the first step can be taken, lies the issue of 'forgiveness is unwarranted'. As long as the belief in 'an eye for a eye' is retained, even the first rung up the ladder must wait.

On the first rung, we are prepared to 'forgive our enemies'. This is real progress as the concept of forgiveness, albeit distorted, has now entered the mind. When we are ready to realise that there are no enemies we will be ready to move further up the ladder. Further misunderstandings about what forgiveness is must be resolved before we can ascend to the rung of 'true forgiveness', which I will refer to as the AAA (Awareness, Acceptance and Asking for help) approach to forgiveness. On reaching the last rung an inner world of peace and joy awaits, a world that nothing outside of ourselves can take away from us.

Forgiveness Exercise (T1a) – Self-forgiveness

The following exercise is available as an audio tape (see Appendix: Recommended Books and Tapes on Forgiveness by Michael Dawson), but you can also dictate it yourself onto a tape, or have it read to you by a friend.

The aim of the exercise is to accept more fully some aspect of yourself that you dislike, or perhaps even hate. As you accept these parts of yourself, they can heal.

Keynote: Whatever you resist persists, whatever you accept will heal.

In this exercise you will be asked at one point to welcome the help that is ever-present for all people all the time, but which we often forget is there: your inner guide, Higher Self, angels, Spirit, Soul, Holy Spirit, God, Jesus, the Goddess, whatever name you give it.

I will use the term 'inner guide' but please feel free to use the name or term you feel most comfortable with. Whatever name you choose, it represents a presence that is all-wise, unconditionally loving, and non-judgemental. It simply seeks to correct your errors of thinking and return to your memory the beauty of who you really are. It is the self you will be when you totally forgive.

This presence sees what we call 'sins' as merely nightmares from which it seeks to awaken us.

Step 1: Relaxation

Make yourself comfortable, either lying or sitting (though the latter is preferable if you think you may snooze off).
* *Take some slow deep breaths.*
* *As you breathe in tense the muscles in both legs, then breathe out and release the tension.*
* *Breathe in and tense the buttocks, breathe out and release the tension.*
* *Breathe in and tense the stomach, breathe out and release the tension.*

• *Breathe in and tense the arms and fists, breathe out and release the tension.*
• *Breathe in and squeeze the shoulder blades together, breathe out and release the tension.*
• *Check that the neck is relaxed – rotate the head if necessary.*
• *Breathe in and tense the face, breathe out and release the tension*
• *Count backwards from 20 to 1 feeling yourself becoming more relaxed as you count.*

Step 2: Asking for Help

You cannot be healed unless you accept help from what I am calling your 'inner guide'.

Send out a prayer to your inner guide in which you welcome and invite its presence to be with you. (The help is always there but needs your invitation, as it will never act against your free will.)

You may wish to imagine this help as a ray of light shining down upon you; as a presence you can feel surrounding you; or as a loving being whose hand you hold.

Step 3: Guided Forgiveness

Recall a time when you experienced yourself acting or thinking in a way that you cannot accept, something you would be ashamed to admit to another.

Perhaps it was hatred, a desire to hurt another or maybe it is something about yourself you dislike such as sadness, weakness, cowardice, lust, pride etc.

PAUSE

Bring it to mind and use one word to describe and label it.

If nothing comes to mind, ask your inner guide to show you an aspect of yourself that needs healing.

Feel where this is mirrored in your body in the form of tension or pain. If it helps, place a comforting and accepting hand over this area.

PAUSE

We will now move into the exercise, which will be in three parts.

For the first part, I will give you a sentence in which you will include your own word (such as hatred, vengeance, lust) and you will then repeat the sentence to yourself in the silence.

The sentence is this:

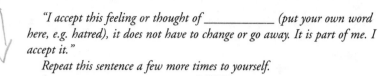

"I accept this feeling or thought of _____ (put your own word here, e.g. hatred), it does not have to change or go away. It is part of me. I accept it."

Repeat this sentence a few more times to yourself.

PAUSE

As you start to repeat the sentence, you may feel a lot of resistance. Just watch this, accept it and notice if it becomes easier with further repetitions. Perhaps you will begin to smile a little at yourself after you repeat this sentence a few times.

PAUSE for one to two minutes

Now see the feeling symbolised as a small, distressed child in front of you. This is not your inner child but a symbol or picture of this feeling. The child may want to talk to you. You have created this experience in your life for a reason. This child can tell you why you have done this. It is important to listen to its story.

PAUSE

Try to comfort the child. It may be angry with you and not want to receive your comfort and reassurance, but just continue to accept it the way it is. You have created this child and in some way it serves you.

PAUSE

See if you can pick the child up and hold it to your heart...dry its eyes ... continue to listen to it.

PAUSE

Are you willing to release what this child symbolises? Is it time for this pain to be released? If you are ready to let part or all of it go ask your inner guide for help. Perhaps some angels are there to lovingly take the child away with them.

If you are not yet ready to release the child, see it grow small enough to put it inside your heart and place it there. Look upon it with acceptance.

PAUSE

Accept how far you have come in this exercise knowing that you can repeat it again.

SUMMARY

- Guilt is the sum total of all our negative thoughts and feelings about ourselves
- Our ego teaches us to deny and project our guilt onto the world
- This dishonest act increases our guilt
- We perceive what we want to see and not what is actually there
- The problem is always in our mind and not in the world
- When we take our projections from the world and back into our minds forgiveness can begin

Chapter Three

THE LADDER OF FORGIVENESS –
THE FIRST RUNGS

False forgiveness

Forgiving our 'enemies'

Forgiveness is unwarranted

FORGIVENESS IS UNWARRANTED

Let us review the meaning of 'forgive', for it is apt to be distorted
and to be perceived as something that entails an unfair sacrifice
of righteous wrath, a gift unjustified and undeserved,
and a complete denial of the truth.

[A Course in Miracles W-pI.134.1:1]

The first obstacle that must be overcome before we can even start to climb the ladder of forgiveness is the thought that forgiveness is unwarranted. As long as this thought is held forgiveness is seen as an undeserved act, which prevents a justified punishment being meted out to our aggressor. Instead, the Old Testament injunction to give "an eye for an eye, and a tooth for a tooth" is thought to be the appropriate response to others' transgressions.

Why is it so hard to forgive? What is the attraction to holding on to our anger? Observations of young children indicate that their anger lasts only a short time. They fight with each other and then usually make up and become friends again. True anger is comparatively short-lived. If it continues over a long period it has been transformed into 'justified vengeance'. Now we cannot let go of our anger otherwise we will let our enemy 'off the hook' and the justified punishment we eventually hope to administer will no longer be forthcoming.

Withholding forgiveness provides us with an excuse not to take full responsibility for our lives if we have suffered in our past. Although painful the memory of the event is deliberately maintained throughout life, allowing us to say to the world, "Don't expect too much of me for I have suffered in the past and will carry the scars until I die". In a while I will share with you a case study that illustrates this very point and also looks at the joy experienced when the old tape in the mind is finally discarded.

There is a deeper and more fundamental reason why we prefer attack to forgiveness. To forgive means to realise that we are similar to the person we accuse – a theme we have explored in previous chapters. Our lack of forgiveness protects us from looking within our own mind to the uncomfortable truths about ourselves. If we cannot forgive we are forced to judge the other person to justify our own lack of forgiveness.[10]

To prevent the discovery of such truths about ourselves we will do anything to pin the blame on the other person. Truth will now mean nothing, as the unforgiving mind tries desperately to maintain its projection onto its perceived enemy. Our minds become closed to any other way of viewing the

---

[10] *A Course in Miracles* W-pII.1.4:4

situation: otherwise the awful truth about ourselves will rise to consciousness. The other person is the sinner and sin deserves punishment.

> If you hate a person, you hate something in him that is part of yourself. What isn't part of ourselves doesn't disturb us.
>
> *[Hermann Hesse]*

It may further be thought that to forgive our enemies would be perceived as an act of weakness and would only encourage further attack. To practice forgiveness does not mean we cannot defend ourselves; what is important is the motivation behind our acts. If our country were being attacked by a cruel, sadistic dictator, it is very likely that after trying all other methods we may be forced to defend ourselves. But here our aim would be to resolve the conflict as soon as possible, with minimum loss of life. Assuming we win the conflict a loving aim would be to restore the attackers' country to a state of harmony, leaving a legacy of goodwill towards us and not the seeds of future conflict.

On some level we realise we are being dishonest, for we are only accusing another of what is in us. This awareness now serves to further increase the guilt we feel. If we turn to the ego for help it will tell us we can get rid of this guilt by getting even angrier with the other person; in the desperate hope that increasing our projection onto the other will solve the problem. A further outburst of anger might feel good temporarily, but will always be followed by further depression as the guilt mounts inside us.

As we look at and judge our enemies, we deliberately filter out the good in them. A world seen as black and white is much more easier to deal with than one with grey areas. Believing the 'other' is wrong and we are right is a thought we would rather not challenge, lest it reveal what we would prefer not to see in ourselves.

The media is well aware of our need for enemies. A quick glance at the best selling tabloids reveals an abundance of stories featuring the misdeeds of others. Banner headlines frequently reveal the crimes or misdemeanors of the famous, offering us the opportunity to gloat over their evils and wish upon them the punishment we secretly feel we deserve. Once again we are off the hook, another enemy has been found to project our guilt onto. Following the advice of our egos we may feel a temporary relief from the burden of our guilt courtesy of the latest scapegoat, but such relief – based on a lie to ourselves – is short-lived. Our guilt increases further from such a dishonest act and our ego counsels us again to get rid of it by finding more enemies to project onto. Thus is perpetuated the ceaseless vicious cycle of guilt and attack which we looked at in Chapter Two.

But what if 'sin' could be seen as 'error' instead? If, on looking within our own mind, we could view what we find so distasteful about ourselves and see it simply as error and not 'sin' the road to forgiveness would be open to us.[11]

If we can have compassion for our errors, we will also have compassion for similar errors in another. What we give to ourselves we also give to others. What we withhold from ourselves we withhold from others.

One definition of sin I particularly like is found in the book *The Initiate* by his pupil – published by Routledge. The book describes an interaction between a disciple and his master. The disciple cannot understand why some people pursue a path of violence in life to which the master replies, "Sin is simply looking for happiness in the wrong directions."

Even dictators are labouring under the illusion that grabbing what they want by force will eventually give them happiness. If we could honestly look at ourselves without judgement, we would see how alike we all are.

One attraction to anger is that it seems like a way in which we can control the behaviour of others. Our hope is that by applying sufficient pressure they will become guilty and conform to our expectations. If we believe attacking another will give us what we want, we must also believe others will think it's a good idea to. This is why we live in fear of being attacked: we believe people will try and do to us what we try to do to them. However, if we choose forgiveness as our path and drop our investment in anger we will lose our sense of vulnerability and find peace instead. To withhold forgiveness from another automatically means we withhold forgiveness from ourselves. As we give so shall we receive, be it love or hate.

---

[11] *A Course in Miracles* Workbook Lesson 134

Case Study – Forgiving Abuse

During my stay at the Findhorn Foundation, I worked for about three years in the healing department. One day a young woman nervously approached me. She said she has some problems and wondered if I could help her. It soon became apparent that she was quite nervous around men and she was quick to admit that her father had sexually abused her when she was five years of age.

Her immediate problem was that for some time her hair had been falling out. We decided to work together on this issue. Early in our session, she saw an image of herself aged five. The child appeared happy and playful and on seeing this she started to cry. This picture reminded her she had known little happiness since the time of the abuse by her father. She had developed a hatred for men, which had been ongoing for 30 years. It was like she had a tape in her mind and each morning she would wake up and press the start button. She could not see that she was using the memory of the abuse to justify the way she felt about life, particularly men. The abuse had actually become something precious to her, which she needed to hold on to. Nobody puts himself or herself through such pain without thinking there is some 'benefit' to them.

In her vision, the little girl took her – the adult – by the hand and led her to the entrance of a house. She was taken upstairs to a room and told to go inside. Awaiting inside was her father. She immediately became angry and sat up. "How could he have done this to me?" she exclaimed. "And my mother knew this was happening but she did not stop it!" She had switched on her 'hate tape'. I said she was free to stop this healing session if she wanted but here was an obvious chance for her to work with something she had painfully held on to for so long. I suggested she might try dialogue with her father, asking him why he had done this to her. She decided to carry on with the session and proceeded to question her father. He explained how, at that time, as well as being married to her mother he also had two mistresses. He said he had felt intimidated by all three women and the only place he could demonstrate any form of power was with her.

For the first time she had some explanation of why the abuse had occurred, and with this was able to relax more. Suddenly, she became very quiet and still. After about five minutes, she started to smile and recounted to me her experience. She said that she had gone to a time before she was born where she was in communication with her father to be. They had great love for each other. In her next life (this one) she wanted to learn more about love, forgiveness and compassion. It was agreed between them that he would sexually abuse her. In this way, she would be given the opportunity to learn a major life lesson of forgiveness and healing. She was obviously very happy at this insight and felt it was right for the healing session to end there.

About two weeks later, I saw her again. She approached me and gave me a hug; the caution and fear I had experienced at our first meeting was gone. She told me her hatred of men had ceased, her hair had stopped falling out, and her anger towards her father had gone. I had not healed her, I had simply given her an opportunity to face a major lesson in her life, to look at her hatred and to let it go: to forgive it.

FORGIVING OUR 'ENEMIES'

We have met the enemy, and it is us.

[Pogo][12]

To move from the position that forgiveness is unwarranted, to the attempt to forgive our enemies is a major step forward. For the first time the concept of forgiveness, albeit in a distorted form, has entered the mind. At least there is now a concept that can be corrected.

To arrive on this rung we have perceived the hopelessness of an 'eye for an eye and a tooth for a tooth' and would rather agree with Mohandas Gandhi when he said, "An eye for eye only ends up making the whole world blind." But we may be left with difficult problems as we try to maintain our new approach. If we are seemingly successful at 'forgiving' our enemies for their

[12] Walt Kelly (cartoonist), Earth Day, 1971.

first transgression, can we maintain this if they continue in their attacks? At some point our patience will be lost and righteous anger will rise once again to the surface, demanding justified retribution.

Some may turn to prayer to help, asking God to help the 'sinners'. Praying for our enemies may seem a noble action, but what is our motivation? Are we asking God to heal the evil ones so they can join the ranks of us, the innocent? We would do better to pray for ourselves so that we no longer see our brother as an enemy.

> The prayer for enemies thus becomes a prayer for your own freedom. Now it is no longer a contradiction in terms. [...] Let it never be forgotten that prayer at any level is always for yourself. [...] Pray truly for your enemies, for herein lies your own salvation. Forgive them for your sins, and you will be forgiven indeed.
>
> *[The Song of Prayer]* [13]

Often people may say they can forgive someone, "but will never forget what they have done," implying they still hold painful memories of the incident. This is a contradiction in terms, as to forgive is to immediately forget all the pain, for we have seen and accepted related behaviour within ourselves.

There is no answer to our failure to maintain forgiveness whilst the enemy is still seen as being outside of us. We want enemies so we can put our sins onto them and so save ourselves the painful awareness of realising how alike we are.

Our investment in needing enemies is huge. Anything and anyone will do to act as a shield to stop us discovering the painful truths of what Jung called our 'shadow side'. We cherish the idea we are innocent because at a deeper level we fear we are not. Our 'innocence' must be defended at all costs and dividing the world into good and bad, guilty and innocent (with me on the innocent side) serves to protect our belief in our innocence.

In treading the path of forgiveness instead of attack, we will come to

---

[13] *The Song of Prayer* (Supplement to *A Course in Miracles*) S-1.II.5:3-4, S-1.II.6:1, S-1.II.6:7-8

realise that our enemies can become our saviours instead of our scapegoats. Without their help, it is very difficult to see what's hidden in our mind that needs healing. There is nothing like having enemies to bring up all the unforgiven thoughts in our minds. They become a superb mirror for what we have tried to bury in our subconscious. In fact, if you brave enough, it would be very educational to spend time with those you normally avoid, and try and watch your reactions to them without judgement. If you find yourself judging what you discover about yourself, you have let the ego return through the back door of your mind. Whether you judge yourself or another does not matter, as either will reinforce the guilt you feel and prevent forgiveness.[14]

> It is impossible to forgive another, for it is only your sins you see in him. You want to see them there, and not in you. That is why forgiveness of another is an illusion [...] Only in someone else can you forgive yourself, for you have called him guilty of your sins, and in him must your innocence now be found. Who but the sinful need to be forgiven? And do not ever think you can see sin in anyone except yourself.
>
> *[The Song of Prayer]* [15]

FALSE FORGIVENESS

The idea of forgiving our enemies can also be included on the next rung of the ladder: false forgiveness. Forgiving our enemies has been discussed separately as it represents a major step, signifying some willingness to look differently at perceived attacks upon ourselves.

The Song of Prayer (supplement to *A Course in Miracles*) describes four different types of false forgiveness,[16] referring to them as different forms of "Forgiveness-to-Destroy". It makes the point that although at times some of them appear charitable, they are all forms of attack and have nothing to do with true forgiveness.

---

[14] *A Course in Miracles* T-11.IV.4:5-5:5

[15] *The Song of Prayer* (Supplement to *A Course in Miracles*) S-2.I.4:2-4, S-2.I.4:6-8

[16] *Ibid.* S-2.II

1. Holier Than Thou

In this form of false forgiveness we take up a position superior in relation to those we regard as transgressing. We are the better people and from our elevated position, we decide to act graciously and forgive others who are perceived as below our 'holy' status. In this attitude of arrogance, we feel our generous offer of forgiveness is really undeserved but out of charity we bestow it upon less worthy others. The true motivation behind this form of 'forgiveness' is to prove that we are superior, more spiritually evolved than those we forgive. If there is not sufficient gain to us, then forgiveness will be withheld.

In this form of false forgiveness, sin is always seen in another and never in us. No responsibility is taken for ourselves for the other is solely to blame. The bad behaviour others exhibit is certainly not in us we say and so we take the high ground and generously forgive them, although they really don't deserve it. Thus we are safely protected from seeing how similar we are to others and can continue to maintain our comfortable image of 'holier than thou'.

2. We Are Both Miserable Sinners

In this form, we no longer assume a superior position to others. Instead, we see ourselves just as sinful as our enemies and both worthy of punishment. This way of thinking can be mistaken for true humility and may produce a 'spiritual competition' over who is the most sinful and humble. Not yet in our awareness is the concept of seeing sin as error that simply needs correction and not judgement and punishment.

3. Martyred Saint

This form of false forgiveness is related to the 'holier than thou' form discussed above. We put on a face, which shows forbearance and meekness when under attack by others. The image we portray to the world is saintly and kindly as we bravely put up with the unjustified attacks upon us. We may even seek opportunities to be martyred under the impression that we are doing God's work as He is asking us to sacrifice ourselves on His behalf. The road to heaven is perceived as one demanding suffering that must be bravely borne with a gentle smile.

"No pain, no gain" is a modern statement of this thought. Although it is very true that we have great opportunities to learn and grow in times of crisis, is it also true that a loving God would demand pain and sacrifice before we could return to a state of peace and joy? Is not this idea of God merely a projection of our own mind, a God created by us based on our own ideas of punishment towards those who upset us?

Beneath the mask of the martyred saint lie feelings of bitterness and pain at the outrage inflicted. "Here am I doing good work and just look at what others are doing to me!" is the silent cry of the martyr. Their suffering face is really an accusing finger pointing at others which declares them guilty and sinful and worthy of God's punishment. Once again evil is seen outside the mind and having nothing to do with ourselves. The very fact that we are feeling angry shows we believe in attack even though we do not openly carry it out.

4. Bargaining and Compromise.

Here we seek to get something in return for our 'gift' of forgiveness. If we find a partner being unfaithful to us we may decide to forgive as long as their behaviour is not repeated. If the partner is caught being unfaithful, again the previous bargain that was struck between you both has been broken and could now result in a withdrawal of forgiveness.

We do not see that what we give we also receive for we must always reinforce in our minds the thoughts we believe in. For example, if we believe we need to cheat to get what we want we must also believe that others value cheating and will try to cheat us. We now spend our lives trying to protect ourselves from others cheating us. If, however, we see that what we do to others we will also do to ourselves we will realise that to give forgiveness unconditionally to others will mean that we will also give it to ourselves.

sυϻϻᴀʀʏ

- To believe in an 'eye for an eye' makes forgiveness appear unjustified and undeserved
- True anger is short-lived. Anger maintained is cultivated vengeance
- We use anger to try to control another
- To forgive is to realise how similar we are to our enemy
- To attack another is a dishonest act that increases our guilt
- There are no sins; only errors to be corrected
- There are no enemies; only our errors looking back at us
- Forgiveness is not a charitable act from a superior to an inferior person
- To believe we are a miserable sinner is to accept the advice of our ego instead of our inner guide
- There is no martyrdom without blame of others
- To use forgiveness as a bargaining tool is to forget that forgiveness is always of ourselves

Chapter Four

The Ladder of Forgiveness – The Last Rungs

True Forgiveness

> Forgiveness recognises what you thought your brother did to you
> has not occurred. It does not pardon sins and make them real.
> It sees there was no sin.
> And in that view are all your sins forgiven.
> *[A Course in Miracles W-pII.1.1:1-4]*

In the preceding chapters, we have explored the question of what needs forgiving. The cause of our pain lies not in the world but in our own minds. Recognising where the problem actually is, enables us to heal it through forgiveness.

True forgiveness begins when we start to realise how similar we are to the person we are trying to forgive. If we cannot forgive what we see in the other, it will be impossible to forgive similar behaviour in ourselves. Other people share our fears, illusions, and inappropriate behaviours and, like us, are often "looking for happiness in the wrong directions". If we realise we are not separate from the one we wish to forgive, then peace becomes possible; our 'enemies' can become our saviours as they mirror what is unhealed within us.

Dr. Kenneth Wapnick has identified in *A Course in Miracles* three steps on the path of forgiveness, which I find helpful in understanding the nature of true forgiveness. I have used these steps as my inspiration for the AAA Approach to forgiveness:

1. *A*wareness and responsibility for the grievance in our minds

2. *A*cceptance and non-judgement of that grievance

and

3. *A*sking inwardly for help to heal the grievance

THE AAA APPROACH TO FORGIVENESS

1. Awareness

Conflict must be resolved. It cannot be evaded, set aside,
denied, disguised, seen somewhere else, called by another name,
or hidden by deceit of any kind, if it would be escaped.
It must be seen exactly as it is, where it is thought to be,
in the reality which has been given it,
and with the purpose that the mind accorded it.
For only then are its defenses lifted,
and the truth can shine upon it as it disappear.

[Ibid. W-pII.333.1:1-4]

Without awareness, the journey of forgiveness cannot begin. Awareness reveals to us what lies in our mind. If we can observe our minds, without any judgement of what we find, we will also allow what is in the unconscious to rise up into the conscious. If we keep observing like this, ever-deeper layers are permitted to rise into our awareness. However, should censoring occur, we will hide the thoughts of which we are ashamed behind a wall of denial. It is this fear of discovering what is hidden in our mind that stops us looking and sets us projecting.

The very fact we get upset at so much of what happens in the world is an indication of the degree to which we have buried what we do not wish to look at in ourselves. The world acts as a mirror to the contents of our unconsciousness. It is easy to be aware of the things we find desirable and bring us pleasure. Whether it is our personal relationships or watching the news that upsets us, both are pointing back to our unconscious. But none of this is easy – otherwise we wouldn't have placed our shameful thoughts in the unconscious in the first place.

> The first steps in self-acceptance are not at all pleasant, for what one sees is not a happy sight. One needs all the courage to go further. What helps is silence. Look at yourself in total silence, do not describe yourself.[17]

We must not underestimate the resistance we all feel to becoming aware of our darker or shadow side. However, by using the world as a mirror to what is unforgiven in our minds we have a golden opportunity to become aware of what we have hidden away in our unconscious. If we do have the willingness to attempt this task we simultaneously call upon our 'inner guide' (see the third A: Asking For Help) to take our ego's projections and use them to show us what we have repressed or denied. In this manner we can 'turn the tables' on our ego and use its very misperceptions to lead us back to what needs forgiving in ourselves.

For most of us, the focus of our awareness is the outer world. We become preoccupied with our job, family, hobbies, relationships, news, events, etc. The demands of our busy modern life seem to require all our attention;

---

[17] *I Am That,* Nisargadatta Maharaj Chetana Press, Bombay.

indeed we may deliberately cultivate busyness to help prevent us from looking at the distress and grievances within. Thus a vicious circle begins, causing our inner pain to increase as we seek more and more ways to escape from it.

To uncover the pain and guilt in our mind we need to develop the role of compassionate witness. By standing back and simply observing what is happening in our mind, we can set ourselves on the road to healing. The very fact we can distance ourselves from our thoughts and simply observe them shows us that we are not those thoughts. We can say, "I have thoughts but I am not my thoughts." To realise that there is a part of our mind that can watch our thoughts is liberating. (see Fig 4.1)

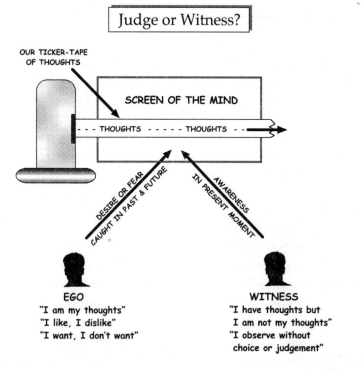

Judge or Witness?

OUR TICKER-TAPE
OF THOUGHTS

SCREEN OF THE MIND

- - - THOUGHTS - - - - - THOUGHTS - -

DESIRE OR FEAR
CAUGHT IN PAST & FUTURE

AWARENESS
IN PRESENT MOMENT

EGO
"I am my thoughts"
"I like, I dislike"
"I want, I don't want"

WITNESS
"I have thoughts but
I am not my thoughts"
"I observe without
choice or judgement"

Fig. 4.1

The watcher or 'compassionate witness' is different from what is being watched and carries with it a sense of being (as in to 'be', to exist, not of being this or that). When the watcher becomes identified with what it is watching, then all our problems begin and we fall into the trap of identifying with negative thoughts and feeling ashamed – even identifying with positive thoughts and feeling pride. Feeling guilty at what we have seen on the screen of our mind will tempt us to deny or try to change it, blocking our way to true healing.

Maintaining attention without identification with the thought processes means the contents of our mind can be revealed to us, allowing the process of forgiveness to continue. Try to become like a scientist who needs to understand some new phenomenon that has been discovered. Judging any observations will limit understanding and distort the findings.

> Start listening to the voice in your head as often as you can. Pay particular attention to any repetitive thought patterns; those old gramophone records that have been playing in your head perhaps for perhaps many years – be there as the witnessing presence. When you listen to that voice, listen to it impartially. That is to say do not judge...for doing so would mean that the same voice has come in again through the back door. You'll soon realize: there is the voice, and here I am listening to it, watching it.
>
> *[Eckhart Tolle]*[18]

Exercise in Awareness

The purpose of this exercise is to practise non-judgemental awareness of the contents of your mind. If this type of practise is new to you don't be surprised at how unruly your mind is. To judge yourself for possessing an undisciplined mind is to follow the unwise counsel of your ego, which can only survive through judgement – of yourself or others.

To help you avoid getting caught up in the first thoughts that come into your mind, and thus losing awareness, I suggest the following:

---

[18] *The Power of Now*, Eckhart Tolle, Namaste Publishing Inc., 1997.

Imagine a house infested with mice who all come and go from one mouse hole. The house owner decides to get a cat to help combat the problem; the cat's job is to wait all day by the mouse hole with its attention fixed on the hole. When a mouse pops its head out of the hole it will immediately notice the cat and will check to see whether the cat has noticed it, or if it is lost in its own feline thoughts. If it finds the cat in an aware state it immediately goes back into the hole. However, if it catches the cat daydreaming it moves out into the house.

In this exercise, I would like you to assume the attitude of an aware cat. However, you will be watching for thoughts to pop up instead of mice. If you are aware enough a thought will last a short time and then subside. This will then be followed by another thought, which you again simply observe without taking any interest in it. You don't have to do anything about the thought, simply watch it without adding to it by thinking about it. If, however, you become interested in the thought your mind will start daydreaming. You might dislike the thought you perceive and judge it, telling yourself you should not think such thoughts. Or, conversely, you might be attracted by the thought and explore it further. Either way you have slipped from simply being aware of thoughts to actively encouraging them. Going back to the analogy of the watching cat, we can see the cat has lapped into an anxious or happy daydream and the house has filled up with mice!

Find a quiet place where you will not be disturbed and sit comfortably with your back upright. Close your eyes and observe the first thought that comes into your mind. At some point an arising thought will have such appeal, either negative or positive, that you will start daydreaming on the theme it presents. In time, you will suddenly realise that your mind is full of thoughts and you have deserted your duty of mind watcher. The next thought might then be, "I am hopeless at this and might as well give up!". Try if you can to simply watch that thought and return to simple awareness of your thinking process. When the exercise feels as if it is becoming too difficult too maintain try to go a further one or two minutes. If after this time the exercise has not become easier then stop.[19]

This exercise clearly indicates to most of us how untrained our minds are. They seem to have a life all of their own. However, the point of this exercise is not to control or stop thoughts, but simply to allow them to be there in your consciousness without judgement.

---

[19] *A Course in Miracles* M-16.4:7-9

By practising this exercise on a regular basis, the attitude of non-judgemental awareness will start to carry over into your daily life. In time you will be rewarded by observing some negative thought or behaviour in yourself and finding you can smile at it and inwardly say, "What's new!" instead of beating yourself up. You will avoid creating further guilt and diminish the likelihood of further repetitions.

Another benefit of this meditative practice is the mind will slowly become less preoccupied with thoughts, leading to an increasing sense of inner peace and well-being. Most people need to practice this over a long period before seeing major results. It's helpful to compare the effort and time required to achieve results in meditation with that required to learn to play a musical instrument well.

2. Acceptance

What you resist persists, what you accept can heal.

The theme of acceptance has already been touched upon above but will now be developed more fully.

Before practicing awareness we will be unaware of much of our motivation for doing things, perhaps ascribing positive reasons for much of our behaviour. A little honest observation of our thoughts and behaviour will likely reveal that some of our motivation is not as noble as we first thought. The ego, as ever, is waiting with its counsel of denial and projection and, if allowed, will force the new insights back into the unconscious. "Ignorance is bliss" it proclaims, but fails to inform us how the submerged problem will now be projected out onto the world where it is safely removed from healing. Without acceptance, judgement follows and forgiveness becomes impossible.

Acceptance of another's inappropriate behaviour is a powerful gift of healing. This does not mean standing by and allowing yourself or others to be hurt; it refers to a non-judgemental awareness and acceptance of the other, seeing their behaviour as a call for help.

To illustrate this let's consider the example of a man who is a compulsive paedophile. He is arrested and brought to trial before a judge who believes the crime is a sin and deserves punishment. The judge has no difficulty in sentencing the man to a long term of imprisonment, hoping that it will incur much suffering for the prisoner. Now consider the same trial but with a judge who does not condemn the man but sees his actions as a call for help. This judge realises the man is at present incapable of controlling his actions and the safety of children is therefore at risk. Further, with each attack upon a child the man is getting increasingly guilty and feeling more and more desperate about a situation that is out of control. For both reasons the judge feels that this man must be put away for his own sake as well as for the children's. The judge's hope is that he can find an institution where there is some possibility of therapy so that with time the prisoner will no longer be a threat to society. The two judges meter out similar sentences but with entirely different motivations.

The power of acceptance is clearly depicted in the film *Son-Rise: A Miracle of Love* (1979), which centres on the true story of Barry and Suzi Kaufman and their autistic three-year-old son Ruan.

At about the age of one Ruan began to withdraw from human contact into his own world. His body developed a rocking motion and he would stretch out his arms and twirl his fingers. Spinning a plate would fascinate him and he would spend long periods of time locked into these behaviours. Ruan was diagnosed as autistic with no hope of recovery. The doctor's advice was to institutionalise him for his own best interests. Barry and Suzi took him for therapy, but were dismayed to find it focused on changing his behaviour through a system of punishment and reward. They withdrew Ruan from therapy and decided to try to help him themselves.

It seemed to Ruan's parents that he did not feel safe in the world and so withdrew into his own self-created universe. This was his haven from an unpredictable and un-accepting world. In order to lure him into the real world they had to make him feel safe and this could never happen if they judged and threatened his inner world. Instead, they decided to show Ruan that he was loved and accepted exactly as he was. To prove this to him they decided to show acceptance by not only allowing his behaviour to continue, but also by sitting in front of him and mimicking his very actions.

The Kaufmans took turns to be with Ruan, spending up to 12 hours at a time with him, seven days a week, for two-and-a-half years. During this period, he started to show signs of coming out of his world by making eye contact with his parents for the very first time. The progress continued and then Ruan suddenly relapsed into his old compulsive behaviour. Undeterred, they continued spending time with him and mimicking his behaviour, until he again started to relate to them and eventually showed no signs of autism at all.

The Kaufmans' 'treatment' of their son was simply based on continuous unconditional acceptance of their son's behaviour. Perhaps few parents of autistic children will have the resources and the time to do what the Kaufmans' did, but nonetheless it is an outstanding example of the power of acceptance.

Exercise in Accepting Another

This is a simple but useful exercise in accepting what another is saying to you.

It will also provide insight into your ability to listen without comment and whether you find it easier to be the one who talks, or the one who listens.

- *Find another person to pair up with.*
- *Sit facing each other and choose who is A and who is B.*
- *A's role is to talk on any subject for five minutes.*
- *B's role is to listen to A without speaking – simply trying to take in and understand what B is meaning.*
- *B must communicate non-verbally that she or he is listening intently to A.*
- *After five minutes B tells A it is time to switch roles.*
- *Don't start any conversation whilst switching roles!*
- *B now talks on any subject for five minutes while A listens attentively in silence.*
- *At the end of five minutes, A tells B that she or he can now stop.*

Take some time to discuss what you learnt from this experience. For exam-
ple, how was it to just listen to another and accept what she or he said? Was
it easier to talk or to listen? Does this reflect your life experience and are you
aware why you prefer one role to another?

One of the difficulties in this second stage of forgiveness is that there is
no point in being aware of our negative thinking if we cannot learn to accept
it. Having seen the futility of pointing an accusing finger at the world, we
should avoid turning the finger around and pointing it at ourselves. There
is a very real danger that with heightened awareness will come an increase in
self-judgement. The ego may now say to us, "Look, I always said you were a
miserable sinner and now I have the evidence!" This is the time to learn to be
kind to ourselves and to develop a sense of humour. If we can learn to smile
gently at our inappropriate thoughts and behaviours this becomes a powerful
act of acceptance, which will start to reduce the guilt we feel; the very guilt
that maintains the problem by encouraging us to resort to denial. Our gentle
smiles whittle away at our pile of guilt and over time our problems diminish
automatically – no longer being fed with self-imposed judgement. If what we
resist persists, it therefore follows that what we accept can heal.

Awareness may reveal thought patterns we have cherished for years
despite the pain they have produced. To accept what we see is to invite healing
and change, and herein lies another problem: we build our lives and identities
around the thoughts we cherish, even the painful ones, and in releasing them
we will lose a part of our identity. Seeing that some of these thoughts do not
serve us, does not mean we can easily accept them and let them go.

Let us take as an example a man who is perceived as kind and helpful,
and who constantly attends to the needs of his friends. He enjoys feeling well
thought of but finds himself nagged by conflicting feelings. On the one hand
he enjoys the appreciation he receives, but on the other he feels his life is not
always his own. He finds it difficult to say "no" to repeated requests for help,
although he is becoming aware that he sends out a message of, "Come to me
for help". One day an insight dawns: he needs people to need him – his self

worth depends on it. In fact, he wants people to be in trouble so he can ride in and save them. After this realisation he no longer sees his actions towards others as helpful, in fact quite the reverse. The message he is really giving out is that other people are weak, cannot help themselves, and will only improve with his help. To carry on rescuing people will maintain his positive image but at a cost of increasing the resentment and guilt he feels. Moreover, he realises most of his friends are caught in 'victim-consciousness' which he has been feeding through his actions.

Aghast at what he now sees as his real motivation, he has arrived at a crucial point in forgiveness. To accept this new insight and let it be healed means his life will change drastically: the response his friends have become used to from him will suddenly change and some of them may not like it. Listening to their calls for help will now be more likely to produce a truly helpful response based on honest reflection and feedback, emphasising that they have their own inner resources to draw on. Helping them to take responsibility for their own lives (as opposed to sorting it all out for them) may not be welcomed though; if his friends are stuck in a 'victim' mode of behaviour they will not appreciate real help and will perhaps view him as hard and unhelpful. Very soon, he may find himself losing friends as they look elsewhere for 'help'.

This is a significant challenge in the second stage of forgiveness. Forgiving ourselves does not affect us solely. Everyone in a co-dependent relationship with us will immediately feel the change we are going through and become alarmed. Strong attempts may be made by others to try to get us back into the old way of relating.

To forgive is to have your life change and we are understandably fearful of that move, but a point is reached when it is simply too painful to hold onto old unproductive thinking and the step is taken. The web of relationships shakes and people may leave, but new ones will also come. Our new friends will welcome our newfound strengths and alliances will form. Now we can look back and see the gains forgiveness has brought into our lives, encouraging us to use and value the tools of awareness and acceptance.

∞∞∞

REFUSAL

I have not been accepting myself today.
I have dug in my heels and refused today.
I have said I won't trade, I won't budge today,
And I'm guilty as hell all the way today.

What brought all this on it's hard to say,
A feeling of turning my mind away,
Of finding some prejudice rearing its head.
When it came to the crunch, it was "No" that I said.

Saying "No" feels quite bad, I'm defending again,
Feeling the doors being shut again.
But somehow attraction is strong to be sad
To jerk about crossly and interact.
It's hard not to judge when you feel this way.
Hard to accept that you want it this way,
For you must, or you wouldn't be feeling this way
All this pain is a choice, strange to say.

Its removal is something I can't do alone.
I can honestly say that I'd rather go Home
Than gnaw like a dog at a meatless bone
And growl at all comers to "LEAVE ME ALONE".

On quiet reflection I'm tired of the pain,
It isn't such hot stuff apportioning blame...
To myself or to others — it's really the same.
Then the help that I asked for JUST CAME!

Minette Quick ©1991

3. Asking for Help

> You do not understand how to overlook errors,
> or you would not make them.
> It would merely be further error to believe either that you do not make
> them, or that you can correct them without a Guide to correction.
>
> *[A Course in Miracles T-9.IV.2:2-4]*

The first two steps in forgiveness are our responsibility. The third step, the removal of the pain and guilt we feel is not of us, but for us.[20] If we are truly willing to see the painful situation we find our self in differently, if we want peace above all else, then a signal for help is sent out to our inner guide. What we call this 'inner guide' is not important.

Asking for help is not a prayer of petition, because help is always here, just waiting to be invited and using words of prayer may not be needed, for what is important is our intention to truly forgive. However, there may be times when a desire to ask our inner guide for help will come and prayer can help focus our intention and illustrate our willingness to be helped. Our prayer of forgiveness might take the form of, "Please show me how to see this situation differently. I want to be at peace now." There are no 'right' words to use; what matters is our intention behind the words.

Lack of forgiveness is like a wall erected against the ever-present light that is shining on us. Forgiveness removes bricks from this wall, letting the light in to do its work of dissolving our unforgiveness and restoring us to peace. We do not understand the ways of spirit, our inner guide, nor do we need to know. What is required of us is a willingness to be helped to see the situation we are in differently. With this invitation, our inner guide can step in and heal our mind.

The idea of surrendering the last part of the process of forgiveness to an invisible power within us will not be welcomed by our egos. After all, by its very nature the ego believes it alone can solve all problems. After living on this

---

[20] *A Course in Miracles* W-pl.23.5

planet for a few years the ego feels it has the experience it needs to handle any situation. What it doesn't accept, is ego got us into trouble in the first place. Without the guidance of a higher part of us we are spiritually blind, trying to live on the advice of our ego. Being blind, we continually 'bump' into situations that cause us pain.

The following book extract describes how Jacques Lusseyran, who was accidentally blinded in both eyes when he was eight years old, came to rely on inner help to navigate his world. Jacques discovered to his surprise that an inner light was available to help him. When walking down a tree-lined road he could sense where the trees were. If he was sufficiently at peace within himself he could even sense where the branches were positioned. When his childhood playmate ran away from him he could still follow her as she left a 'red trail' behind her. The book also illustrates how he could lose touch with this guidance. His story mirrors our own lives and our spiritual blindness when we try to do everything by ourselves.

Still, there were times when the light faded, almost to the point of disappearing. It happened every time I was afraid.

If, instead of letting myself be carried along by confidence and throwing myself into things, I hesitated, calculated, thought about the wall, the half-open door, the key in the lock; if I said to myself that all these things were hostile and about to strike or scratch, then without exception I hit or wounded myself. The only easy way to move around the house, the garden or the beach was by not thinking about it at all, or thinking as little as possible. Then I moved between obstacles the way they say bats do. What the loss of my eyes had not accomplished was brought about by fear. It made me blind.

Anger and impatience had the same effect, throwing everything into confusion. The minute before I knew just where everything in the room was, but if I got angry, things got angrier than I. They went and hid in the most unlikely corners, mixed themselves up, turned turtle, muttered like crazy men and looked wild. As for me, I no longer knew where to put hand or foot. Everything hurt me. This mechanism worked so well that I became cautious.

When I was playing with my small companions, if I suddenly grew anxious to win, to be first at all costs, then all at once I could see nothing. Literally, I went into fog or smoke.

I could no longer afford to be jealous or unfriendly, because, as soon as I was, a bandage came down over my eyes, and I was bound hand and foot and cast aside. All at once a black hole opened, and I was helpless inside it. But when I was happy and serene, approached people with confidence and thought well of them, I was rewarded with light. So is it surprising that I loved friendship and harmony when I was very young?

Armed with such a tool, why should I need a moral code? For me this tool took the place of red and green lights. I always knew where the road was open and where it was closed. I had only to look at the bright signal which taught me how to live.

[From And There Was Light] [21]

The inner light that guided Jaques also helped him discern whom he could trust and whom he could not. This talent helped him become the leader of a large group of French resistance fighters in the Second World War. The one time he went against this inner knowing resulted in him being arrested and imprisoned in a concentration camp. His reliance on his inner guide allowed him to survive the harsh conditions of the camp and to go on to become a university professor after the war.

When we learn to relax and trust the guidance we have within, we open up a new and wonderful path in life. Not continually relying on our past experience to sort out our present problems allows a heavy burden to fall from our shoulders. At first the ego will often dress up in the inner guide's clothes and offer us the answers we may prefer to hear, but through a process of trial and error we will start to discern the small, quiet voice within. The hallmark of following true inner guidance is a peaceful outcome.

The inner guide will choose the form the forgiveness must take. Perhaps we will feel led to talk or write to the person we have problems with, or it may be more appropriate to offer a prayer instead and not to approach the person

[21] *And There Was Light – The autobiography of a blind hero in the French Resistance* by Jacques Lusseyran. Floris Books, 1963

at all. This decision is too complex for us and must be left in the hands of our inner guide. We are being asked not to run the whole show, but to do our part by not pointing the accusing finger at ourselves or others and then allowing our inner guidance to choose the form the forgiveness takes.

> Now can He (the guide) make your footsteps sure, your words sincere; not with your own sincerity, but with His Own. Let Him take charge of how you would forgive, and each occasion then will be to you another step to Heaven and to peace. [...] He knows the need; the question and the answer. He will say exactly what to do, in words that you can understand and you can also use. Do not confuse His function with your own. He is the Answer. You the one who hears.
>
> *[Song of Prayer]*[22]

The AAA Forgiveness Exercise

Use this exercise at any time you lose your peace. It utilises the principles of awareness, self-acceptance and asking for help – the three A's.

In the exercise you will be asked at one point to welcome the help that is ever-present for all people all the time, the help we often forget is there.

This help may be known by many names: your inner guide, Higher Self, angels, Spirit, soul, Holy Spirit, God, Jesus, the Goddess. I will use the term inner guide but please feel free to use whatever name or term you feel most comfortable with.

This symbol represents a presence that is all wise and loving with absolutely no judgement of you. This presence sees what you may call 'sins' as merely nightmares which it seeks to awaken you from. It simply seeks to correct your errors of thinking and return to your memory the beauty of who you really are. It is the self you will be when you totally forgive.

---

[22] *Song of Prayer* S-2.III.3:3-4, S-2.III.5:6-9

Step 1: Relaxation
• *Make yourself comfortable, either lying or sitting (though the latter is preferable if you think you may snooze off).*
• *Take some slow deep breaths.*
• *As you breathe in tense the muscles in both legs, then breathe out and release the tension.*
• *Breathe in and tense the buttocks, breathe out and release the tension.*
• *Breathe in and tense the stomach, breathe out and release the tension.*
• *Breathe in and tense the arms and fists, breathe out and release the tension.*
• *Breathe in and squeeze the shoulder blades together, breathe out and release the tension.*
• *Check that the neck is relaxed – rotate the head if necessary.*
• *Breathe in and tense the face, breathe out and release the tension*
• *Count backwards from 20 to 1 feeling yourself becoming more relaxed as you count.*

Step 2: Asking for Help
   Send out a prayer to your inner guide in which you welcome and invite its presence to be with you. (The help is always there but needs your invitation, as it will never act against your free will.)
   You may wish to imagine this help as a ray of light shining down upon you; as a presence you can feel surrounding you; or as a loving being whose hand you hold.

Step 3: Guided Forgiveness
   It is important in this exercise that you don't try to heal yourself. Your job is to invite the healing in and you can do this by fully accepting your pain and asking sincerely for help.
   Bring into your awareness the person or situation you wish to forgive. Relive the memory of the event you find distressing. Allow the feeling to come with that memory.
   Become aware of the area of your body where you're feeling tense, anxious, angry, or fearful, etc. Place one or two hands gently over that area.
   Begin the awareness process by observing the pain: what is its size and shape? Where does the tension start and where does it stop? How deep does this tension go into your body? Is it mainly on the surface, or does it penetrate deeper? Does it have a colour? Is the colour uniform? Is this area hotter or

colder than the rest of the body? Does this area feel hard or soft, or some other texture? (If necessary, you can repeat the above questions until you feel you know and accept this part of your body.)

Do you wish to retain this pain, or are you willing to let it go?

If you are not yet willing to release this pain then gently accept this fact and tell your self you can always repeat this exercise another time.

If you have decided this pain no longer serves you, you are now at the stage where you can ask for help to let the pain go. Say to yourself, "I am willing to to let this pain go. Please help me." This is your call to your inner guide who will respond in a way that is appropriate for your healing. Your job now is to simply relax and trust the process. Nor do you know the time of your healing – leave that to the guide.

It is your intention that is important here. Having accepted that this pain is self-created, that you're willing to let it go, you call upon the help that is always there for you. At this stage, you must let all your grievances go. You are no longer concerned with the situation or the person that seemed to cause the pain you feel; you have taken responsibility for the way you feel; you have taken your projections back from the world. Now you can decide to let your pain go.

This is a gentle process; there should be no sense of urgency. Tell yourself it is OK to feel this pain – encourage acceptance of yourself instead of judgement. Anything you resist will persist, but anything you accept can heal. If you begin to feel a decrease in pain, you know your prayers have been sincere. Just as you chose the pain in the first place, you now choose to let it go. If the pain does not go away, then there is a part of you that still finds it of value. Try not to condemn yourself over this. Feel free to try this exercise again at a later time.

SUMMARY

AAA Approach to Forgiveness

1. AWARENESS

- What is denied cannot be forgiven.
- Awareness of our inner world is as important as awareness of our outer world.
- Our egos will fight our attempts to become more aware of our darker sides.
- Watch thoughts without judgement – develop a 'compassionate witness'.
- The ability to watch thinking means we are not our thoughts.

2. ACCEPTANCE

- What you resist persists.
- Acceptance dissolves guilt.
- Acceptance invites healing and change.
- Change is feared and can block forgiveness.

3. ASKING FOR HELP

- Steps one (awareness) and two (acceptance) are our responsibility.
- A genuine desire for peace invites healing.
- Our inner guide completes the forgiveness process and will choose the form forgiveness takes: our job is to surrender to its guidance

CALL FOR LOVE

When we refuse to forgive and attack others instead, what are we teaching ourselves? We are teaching ourselves daily by what we say, do and think. If we keep telling ourselves we are weak, we will become weaker. If we attack others, we teach ourselves hate is more powerful than love. Similarly, if we tell ourselves we are supported by an inner love and wisdom we will grow more secure and confident.

If another person attacks us, we have a choice of two responses: to attack/defend, or to see their actions as a call for love, which asks for our understanding and help.

> Every loving thought is true. Everything else is an appeal
> for healing and help, regardless of the form it takes.
> Can anyone be justified in responding with anger to a brother's plea
> for help? No response can be appropriate except the willingness
> to give it to him, for this and only this is what he is asking for.
> *[A Course in Miracles T-12.1.3:3-6]*

If we choose attack or defence we are saying to ourselves, "I am weak and need defence. I do not believe I should help my attacker and therefore I do not believe there is help available for me". Our response denies help to both of us; the more we defend, the weaker and more isolated we feel. What we do to others we also do to ourselves. It is therefore 'divine selfishness' to see another's attack as a call for our help. As we return love for attack, we reinforce in our minds that we are strong, in need of no defence and have inner resources to guide us. We see that in defencelessness our safety lies.[23]

None of the above refers to what form our behaviour takes when under attack. If we have advanced far enough along the path of forgiveness, this will not concern us. We will simply know how best to respond in any given situation. Our inner guide will tell us what to do or say and we may safely leave all of that up to its wisdom and love.

---
[23] *A Course in Miracles* Lessons 135, 153

The more we practise this the more we realise it works. This is true forgiveness and demonstrates that attack has no effect upon us. Instead, it provides an opportunity to strengthen the awareness of the love and wisdom we all carry within us. As mentioned earlier, our attacker can be turned into our saviour.[24]

No longer do we believe that another must lose for us to win, instead we see that to give is to receive, and so we happily extend our love and wisdom knowing that we automatically reinforce them in our own mind.[25]

NOTHING TO FORGIVE

This last rung on the ladder of forgiveness will not be reached until true forgiveness has been mastered and becomes a habitual response to challenges in life. The constant practice of forgiveness chips away at our mountain of guilt and bit by bit we recognise the things we dislike in ourselves and cease projecting them onto others. As the darker, deeper layers in our unconscious reveal themselves, we are now better prepared to accept them and let them go. This is not to say that the journey is easy, for 'dark nights of the soul' are still likely to await us on the path.

As we start to master forgiveness more of our day will be spent guided by the love and wisdom of spirit and less by our ego. A day will arrive when we fully accept that love is our true nature, and unity – not the ego – is our reality. At that moment, our belief in the ego will vanish and it will be no more. We will realise our oneness with all things and attain peace. With the ego gone there is nothing to deny and project onto the world, and hence nothing to forgive.

Before we realise our true spiritual identity we must be prepared for the attacks of the ego, which is literally fighting for its life. As we have previously falsely identified ourselves with the thoughts of the ego, there will be times when our egos try and reclaim their lost ground.

---

[24] *Ibid.* W-pl.16.1.12:6
[25] *Ibid.* T-25.VII.12

The ego will not go without pitting all its cunning against us. The ego is a thought we have created and, like any creation, it wants to live. As we move further into the experience of oneness and away from the appeal of separation and individuality, the ego, which is simply the thought of separation, will do everything in its power to dissuade us. But what we gain on this journey fortifies us for the road ahead and no one can fail in the end. The appeal of love will finally win over selfishness.

Tolerance for pain may be high, but it is not without limit.
Eventually everyone begins to recognize, however dimly,
that there must be a better way. As this recognition becomes more firmly
established, it becomes a turning point.

[Ibid][26]

The loss of personal identity, that we are a separate identity in a body, is a terrifying prospect and our egos will tell us there will be nothing left if we let the ego go. "How can you manage to run your daily life without my experience and judgement!" it declares. "Without me all will be chaos."

Behind our ego's thoughts of defence and attack, is a loving and wise part of us – our spiritual reality – just waiting to take over our lives and effortlessly guide us through our days. The journey of forgiveness must be a gradual one, allowing us to move at a pace that will not terrify us. A sudden unexpected loss of the ego can do more harm than good if we are not sufficiently prepared. The gradual lessening of the guilt in our minds through forgiveness provides the preparation we need.

We begin the inner journey with firm convictions of who we are and our roles in life but find as the journey progresses we become less sure until we are no longer certain of anything. The ego seems so solid and real, but with time it becomes transparent. The following story is helpful in understanding the illusory nature of the ego:

---

[26] *Ibid.* T-2.III.3:5-7

In a small village lived a cow herder named John. Each morning he would go into the cow shed and untie the ropes around the necks of the cows. (Without this restraint the cows would wander away from the shed and get lost.) John would then lead the cows out to pasture. At night he would bring the cows back to the shed and retie their ropes. One evening he was shocked to discover that a rope was missing. Fearful that a cow might get lost overnight he sought the help of an elder in the village. John was told there was no problem. All he had to do was to go back to the shed and pretend to tie up the last cow. John returned to the shed and followed this instruction.

The following morning he nervously approached the cowshed wondering what he might find. To his relief the cow with the non-existent rope around its neck was standing in line like all the others. He quickly untied the remaining cows and led them all out to graze. As usual he counted the number of cattle that were in the field. To his horror he discovered there was one missing. He searched everywhere but could not locate the animal. But then he had a hunch and went back to the cow shed where he found the cow he had tied up with a non-existent rope still standing there. John tried to lead the cow out of the shed. Although the cow was very willing to follow John it could not move because of its 'rope'.

John returned to the village elder and told him the story. The advice this time was to return to the cow and pretend to take the rope off its neck. Once that was achieved the cow happily left the shed to join the others.

[adapted from Awaken Children! by Mata Amritanandamayi]

In this story the rope symbolises the ego. Just like the rope, the ego does not actually exist. However, we believe it does and so it seems very real to us and we allow its thought system of denial and projection to exert itself in our minds. While we maintain the belief that the ego is necessary to our survival the guidance of our true self must wait.

The ego is like the darkness in a room where all the windows are shuttered. Once the windows are opened, the light shines away the darkness. The darkness is not real in itself; it is simply the absence of light.

The FRUITS OF FORGIVENESS

Forgiveness will open the shutters of the mind and let the love and wisdom of our inner selves shine in, causing the ego to vanish. Our inner guide now takes over the role we once asked the ego to perform. On this happy day the realisation that "I need do nothing" will dawn upon our minds.

> When peace comes at last to those who wrestle with temptation
> and fight against the giving in to sin;
> when the light comes at last into the mind given to contemplation;
> or when the goal is finally achieved by anyone,
> it always comes with just one happy realization; 'I need do nothing.'
> [A Course in Miracles] [27]

Now we will effortlessly know what to say, what to do and where to go at any time. Jiddu Krishnamurti once said, "Only confused people have choices." In any situation there is only one right answer and our inner wisdom knows what that is.

When we at last finish our journey of forgiveness and no sense of sin, guilt or fear remains in our minds, and then there will be nothing left to project out onto others. We will look out onto a forgiven world. Previously the world had been a screen for our projections, so with no guilt to project the world we see will be transformed. The world's activities will not have changed, but our perception of them will. Now we will see all events in the world from a much simpler perspective. People will be seen as either extending love to others or asking for it. [28] There will be nothing in between. Forgiveness is now seen as an illusion, but a necessary one to help us out of our dream of separation.

Becoming peaceful does not guarantee us freedom from attacks by others. Our very peace can provoke attack, as was amply demonstrated in the life of Jesus. The ego mind perceives everyone as sinners and worthy of

[27] Ibid. T-18.VII.5-7
[28] Ibid. T-12.I.3:3-7

judgement and attack; seeing someone at peace contradicts its thought system and undermines its security. The resulting fear provokes the ego to attack. However, such attacks, whether physical or psychological, can have no effect on someone who has relinquished their ego: there is nothing left to strike back. Instead the attack is seen as an appeal for healing which will be given, whether accepted or not.

By being defenceless you are saying, "Your attack has no effect on me, you can only attack my ego, but that has now gone, it was never real anyway. And if my ego was not real then neither is yours." This gift may not be received now but waits for a time when the other person is ready for it. No love is ever lost.

Daily practice

How long our journey of forgiveness takes depends on our willingness to dedicate our days to finding peace. Daily priorities often revolve around accomplishing a worldly goal rather than an inner goal. However, if we can work on both the outer and the inner levels simultaneously our progress will be immeasurably advanced. The following suggested daily practice embraces this way of approaching our lives.

As you awake in the morning set the purpose of your day: to find peace in all situations you encounter. For example, if you need to talk to your boss about a pay rise, the first priority is to try to be at peace with your boss rather than the hoped-for outcome of the interview. In all situations that require some practical steps to be taken, you approach on two levels. Level one, the first priority, is to seek and find peace in the situation. Level two, the second priority, is achieving the goal – if possible.

Another example could be sickness. You try different ways to get better (second priority) but seek, with the help of your inner guide, to remain at peace (first priority) no matter whether you get better or not.

Attaining and keeping peace now becomes the **purpose** of everything you do during the day – it is your first priority. It does not matter what happens, as you now view all happenings as classrooms wherein you can learn forgiveness and truth, and therefore attain peace. You could even find yourself in disastrous circumstances (according to your ego) such as a car crash, but if finding peace remains your first priority, the situation can become a blessing. This is not easy to do, as your ego will encourage you to view such a situation from the standpoint of a justified victim.

> It takes great learning to understand that all things, events,
> encounters and circumstances are helpful.
> *[A Course in Miracles]*[29]

Although one part of you is looking for ways to find peace and joy there is still likely to be a powerful identification with the mind of your ego. We retain a strong desire to be a separate, unique individual who is different from others and wishes to be self-sufficient and in sole control of his or her life.

As you follow these steps to finding peace this desire will always act in opposition and attempt – often successfully – to draw you back to the advice of the ego, which is terrified of the new direction you are undertaking. Why terrified? Because as you move along on this journey love will gradually shine away the ego – and therefore your individuality.

> And if you find resistance strong and dedication weak,
> you are not ready. Do not fight yourself.
> *[Ibid]* [30]

Instead, forgive yourself for not forgiving; forgive yourself for not truly wanting peace and preferring your ego instead. You are not as far along the spiritual path as you perhaps once thought or hoped. With this knowledge, learn to smile at your ego and its desire to be separate. This is wonderful progress, such an approach will diminish the guilt that keeps you from finding inner peace.

[29] *Ibid.* M-4.I.4-5
[30] *Ibid.* T-30.I.1:6-7

SUMMARY

- Attacking others increases our vulnerability
- Attacks from others are a call for help
- What we give to others we reinforce in our own mind (love or hate)
- The ego is an illusion we choose to believe in
- When the ego is finally transcended the need for forgiveness is over
- Peace and quiet joy await us at the end of our journey of forgiveness

Chapter Five

HELPING OTHERS TO FORGIVE

I am here only to be truly helpful.
I am here to represent Him who sent me.
I do not have to worry about what to say or do,
because He who sent me will direct me.
I am content to be wherever He wishes
knowing He goes there with me.
I will be healed as I let Him teach me to heal.

[A Course in Miracles T-2.V.18:2-6]

WORKING WITH OTHERS

This chapter enables me to share with other people – especially those involved
with counselling and therapy – an overview of some of the ideas and techniques I have found helpful in trying to facilitate others to forgive themselves.
However, the case histories I have included in order to illustrate the techniques
used may be of value to all – therapists or not. I assume that anyone drawn to
trying these approaches will already have received training in psychotherapy.

A healing technique is of secondary importance compared with the presence of the therapist. By 'presence', I am referring to the therapist's state of

mind whilst working with a client. For healing to occur therapists need to be guided from within, and this can only happen if they are at peace around the client. A wonderful healing technique used at the wrong moment is useless. Knowing when to speak or remain silent, when to use a different approach or method, must be guided from a place higher than reason and logic. Therapeutic skill needs to be combined with inner listening. The following account of a therapy session conducted by Dr. Kenneth Wapnick illustrates this point:

One of my first therapy experiences after I began working with the Course in Miracles afforded me a powerful example of the relationship between healing and forgiveness. I had seen Sister Annette for about two months. She was fifty years old and had been in religious life almost thirty years. She was also one of the angriest people I had ever worked with, filled with a silent hatred toward those in authority that would have destroyed mountains. Over the first few sessions, Sister Annette was able to begin questioning some of her attitudes toward her Order and her desire for revenge. She no longer seemed quite as committed to the retaliative steps she had contemplated. Or so I thought. One day Annette walked into the office with her face coldly exhibiting the 'wrath of God!' Her convent co-ordinator had done something she judged as being beyond forgiveness, and Sister Annette was hell bent on war, absolutely closed to any suggestions she do otherwise.

That same morning I had come down with a very bad cold and felt miserable. Not all my prayers and meditation were able to shift this, and I sat before Annette feeling utterly helpless and discouraged. I knew that if she left me as she had come in, she would be making an irrevocable mistake she would regret the rest of her life. Yet nothing I said could budge her, and my growing frustration only made my cold worse. The more frustrated I became, the more real I made Annette's angry symptoms and, correspondingly, my own as well. Obviously, I was projecting my unforgiveness of myself onto Annette, seeing in her stubborn clinging to her anger the mirror of my stubborn clinging to my cold, not to mention my own failure as a therapist. Separation through our symptoms became reinforced, and healing through joining retreated still further behind clouds of guilt and anger.

What added to my difficulty was the belief that Annette had been sent to me from God, and as she was in serious trouble it was my responsibility to help her. And I was obviously failing. About midway through the session, my desperation led me finally to remember that I was not the Therapist, and that I certainly could not be more concerned for Annette than Jesus was. Even as I was talking and listening to her, in another part of my mind I began to pray for help, asking Jesus to provide the words that would heal her anger and fear, and restore to her awareness the love that was her true identity.

The response was immediate, and I suddenly became available to the help that was there – for me. A warm surge of energy rose up from my chest, through my lungs, nose and throat, and I could feel my cold being healed and my head clearing up. At the same time I began to speak. I don't recall what I said, and doubt if it were anything too different from what I had said previously. Only now I was different. I no longer saw Annette as separate from me, a patient in trouble whom I, as therapist, had to help. She now was my sister, and by joining with her I was joining with Jesus. I had become the patient as well, and together we received healing from the forgiving love of God. By the end of the session, her softened face reflected the shift from anger and fear to forgiveness and love, as my well being reflected the same shift in myself. I had learned my lesson that day, to be relearned many times thereafter.[31]

∞∞∞

Without the help of an inner guide, it is impossible to work out what is best for the client. Fortunately, we all have access to this wisdom once we can relax and be willing to be helped from that source. The therapist needs to be peaceful to access this inner wisdom.

If therapists find the presence of their clients disturbing, then their first duty is to restore their own peace of mind before attempting to help their

---

[31] *Forgiveness and Jesus* by Dr. Kenneth Wapnick. Published by *Foundation For A Course In Miracles* © 1983 See Appendix 2 for book description.

clients. To achieve this they need to honestly admit they have lost their peace, that the client is not responsible for this and they could do with some help to see the situation differently. If their intention is sincere, they can rest assured the inner help will come.

When clients are in the presence of therapists who are at peace they are given a message that they are not being judged, that they are not being seen as a sinner. This provides an opportunity for clients to change their minds and release the burden of self-imposed guilt.

In the previous account of a counselling session, Dr. Kenneth Wapnick describes the turning point in the session as the moment he began to ask for help, in his case praying to Jesus. No longer knowing how to help he turned within for guidance and received the help, both for himself and for his client.

The following is a summary of some of the techniques I use when helping others to forgive and heal themselves. I think of these healing approaches as keys on a piano. I need to know these keys well, but try to allow a higher part of myself to know when to play them. Therapeutic training enabled me to practise particular keys well (for example, guided visualisation), but it is only through happily surrendering to a wisdom beyond my personality that the appropriate keys get pressed at the right moment.

A therapist does not heal; he lets healing be.
He can point to darkness but he cannot bring light of himself,
for light is not of him. Yet, being for him, it must also be for his patient.
The Holy Spirit is the only Therapist.
He makes healing clear in any situation in which He is the Guide.
You can only let Him fulfil His function. He needs no help for this.
He will tell you exactly what to do to help anyone He sends to you for help,
and will speak to him through you if you do not interfere.
[A Course in Miracles][32]

∞ ∞ ∞

---

[32] *A Course in Miracles* T-9.V.8:1-8

SUMMARY Of TECHNIQUES TO hELP OTHERS FORGIVE ThEMSELVES

Each summary is followed by an illustrative case history. Please note that not all my healing sessions are as 'effective' as those that follow, as there are always three factors involved. Firstly, there is the level of therapeutic skill of the therapist. Secondly, the ability of the therapist to give from his or her highest source and thirdly, the client's genuine willingness to change and receive help. After a successful session, both client and therapist feel they have received a gift.

1. Initial Prayer

Both therapist and client ask that healing is given and that insight is received into what the client needs to change in his or her life to bring about a lasting healing. The prayer is usually silent and takes the form of a welcome; an openness to receive the healing that is always there for us. It is an act of surrender to a wisdom greater than our every day intelligence.

Mary was in a weak state and had been confined to bed for a few days. She had asked me to see her as she had discomfort in the area of her womb. After the initial relaxation stage, we both uttered a silent prayer. After a few minutes silence, feeling ready to start the session, I asked Mary what was happening for her. Little did I know that the work had already started: she told me how after the prayer she moved immediately into a quiet and deep space within. "I was shown how I have been strongly resisting certain lessons in a relationship that I am currently in. These lessons were very clear and I had to decide to accept them and stop getting upset with my partner. I said that I would and I meant it. Immediately the discomfort in my womb starting to melt away." She felt complete with the session and so we stopped there. Mary told me later that the following day she was well enough to leave her bed.

This incident shows how quick healing can be if we are ready to accept help and willing to change our minds about what we perceive the problem to be. It was a powerful demonstration that healing does not need time but simply acceptance. Healing is already waiting to come to us and simply awaits our willingness to receive it; delays are caused by us resisting the moment of healing.

2. Visualisation

If the client has a physical problem, ask them to describe the area to you. Ask questions that encourage the client to explore how they see or feel the area, for instance:

> "How large is the area?"
> "What shape is it?"
> "What colour is it?"
> "How deep does it go into the body?"
> "Is it hard or soft in texture?"
> "Is it warm or cold?"
> "Does it remind you of some kind of object?"

Such questioning encourages the client to observe and thereby accept a part of the body that previously he or she may have been resisting. Remember: What you resist persists; what you accept can change and be healed.

The body's pain has a message, and the above procedure is like welcoming the messenger and seeing what 'clothes' it is wearing. You can now ask, "What feelings (not thoughts) does this area have?" The client may, for example, describe the area as a hard red ball, which feels angry. This feeling is the voice of the messenger. Encourage the client to stay with the feeling and see where it leads them. The feeling can be asked to speak out loud directly to the client and tell its story (see following Tracking Back section). In this way, the physical pain can act as a door to denied and unforgiven thoughts.

Jean had confined herself to bed because her ears were giving her considerable pain. The condition had been ongoing for many years. We spent some time exploring and accepting the pain in her ears. Suddenly, a picture of her childhood home appeared to Jean: she was standing by a door watching her parents argue heatedly and at one point her mother's glasses fell to the floor. Jean felt this scene must have been a very painful experience as she saw herself cover her ears and run off to be with her sister. I encouraged Jean to talk out loud to her mother as if she were in the room and tell her of her feelings. In this way, long-suppressed feelings have a chance of being expressed and released. Jean then experienced a pain in her side, a condition she had also suffered for many years. She next saw herself in the bathroom up against the bath, being kicked in the side by her father. As she re-experienced the scene the pain left her side and moved into her right arm. The scene of the quarrel between her parents returned. As she once again watched them quarrel Jean felt motivated to pick up her mother's glasses from the floor with her right arm and offer them to her mother. As she did, the pain left her arm. The following day Jean was able to leave her bed with her condition improved.

3. Tracking Back

When an emotion connected with the problem (physical or psychological) arises, but there is no corresponding insight, encourage the client to stay in the emotion and facilitate them going back in time to the origin of the problem. This is a powerful technique that can sometimes take the person to a previous life. It is important to keep the client in their feelings and out of their logical minds. Ask questions such as:

"What does it feel like?"
"Does this remind you of anything?"
"How old are you?"
"Where are you?"
"How were your father and mother for you?"
"Where does this feeling take you?"

Always use open-ended questions as opposed to closed questions that generate a "Yes" or "No" answer and no more.

Example:

Open-ended question: "How was your relationship with your father?"
Closed question: "Did you like your father?"

Hold the client to the image. It is important to trust the process. There should be no pressure from the therapist to find a solution. Go from the present clues to the past and follow the images. Follow what the client gives. Work with his or her symbols and language. And do not try to force the client to an earlier life, if that is needed it will spontaneously happen.

(See Chapter Two – Forgiveness and Sickness for an example of this approach.)

4. Spontaneous Inner Journey

After relaxation, clients may start on a spontaneous inner journey of discovery. The client may see him or herself going on a journey – images of tunnels, dark places, water, mountains, wise and dark beings being common. The client may or may not want to share what is happening, but will need your caring and attentive presence. If the client is silent you can check in from time to time to see if they want to share anything of the experience. And if the client gets stuck or scared on their journey you can facilitate it with your encouragement. You can suggest asking for help, maybe asking the inner guide, a wise being, or an angel to assist (see next section Asking for Help).

The following account occurred while I was living at the Findhorn Foundation. It was late in the evening and I was just about to retire when a tearful young woman needing a healing session approached me. Although I felt tired, it did feel right to say yes to her request.

Kate had been wandering around the woodland outside the college, feeling that she had lost trust with life. Early on in the session, she spontaneously started on an inner journey. Entering through some doors she descended a staircase into darkness, but fearing what might be there, she could go no further. I suggested she might ask for help and she was rewarded by the appearance of a being holding a light. Her journey proceeded through tunnels, which led to a forest where a cliff eventually stopped her. I had been silent throughout most of this journey and was feeling quite tired by now. I did not feel very connected with Kate and her silent experience. She then said, "I am stuck on my journey. There is a cliff I need to scale but feel you are no longer with me". Her feedback to me was accurate: it was after midnight and sleep was calling me. However, I refocused my energies and suggested she visualise a ladder with us both climbing it. Her journey recommenced until eventually she arrived at the top of a mountain. Here she experienced a strong feeling of peace and felt all the negativity she had been carrying melt away. I met Kate a few days later. She told me, "I feel I can trust life again."

This session taught me that even if the client called for only minimal facilitation, my ongoing supportive presence was still a necessity. I still needed to be on that journey with her, even as a silent partner.

5. Asking for Help

Powerful assistance can be obtained for the client by asking or praying for help during the healing session. The client will often experience the help as a particular visual image to which he or she can relate, indeed the beings who may appear can sometimes guide the rest of the session and become the most transformative part of the healing. They may appear in many forms, as friends, wise beings, angels, or animals. It is important to tell the client that these helpers will not go against the free will of human beings and must therefore be consciously asked to attend the healing session. They do not come where they are not invited. You may wish to suggest that the client imagine a beautiful place in nature where they can meet a being who will be of help (see below, 6. Guided Journey)

During the early part of a workshop I was giving, I led the group on a guided inner journey. The object of the exercise was to connect the workshop participants more closely with their own inner source of wisdom.

After a period of relaxation and guided imagery, I hoped they would meet a wise and loving being with whom they could talk and receive advice. Towards the end of this exercise, I noticed that a young woman in the group had obviously terminated this exercise early. Later that day Mary complained that her right arm was hurting her and it was found that by putting her arm in a sling her pain was relieved. The following day Mary complained that the vision in her right eye was getting worse and eventually that eye required a patch and a bandage. I asked Mary what had happened on the guided journey we had done the previous day. She told me she did not meet a white being, whom she hoped for, instead, a dark figure showed up. This so frightened her she stopped the exercise. I told her that dark beings can be equally useful as they can teach us about our shadow side, the darker areas in our unconscious. I inquired if she wanted to repeat the journey but she declined.

The next day Mary's other eye began to suffer. She said if felt like looking out of a slit in a window. Although by now we were all getting quite concerned about her she was resistant to any offer of healing. During a further exercise she told me that an inner voice spoke to her. It said, "Now is the time to look inside". When I asked her if she was willing to do this she again refused help. A few days later she finally approached me and asked for a private healing session. I repeated the exercise I had used earlier with the group: the guided journey to meet a wise being. This time she met two beings, a white one, and a black one. Unlike last time, she did not panic but waited to see what would unfold. She began to relive what appeared to be an earlier episode in her life: she was looking for a razor blade and, on finding it, tested its sharpness on a piece of paper. It soon became apparent that she was reliving a previous suicide attempt. The scene faded and she became quiet again.

I suggested she ask these beings to show her anything she needed to let go, to forgive. She was next shown a scene in a train carriage. It was dark and crowded; the people were very afraid and talking about camps. After a long journey the train stopped and the doors were opened from outside. They were forced to leave the carriage and step-by-step she recounted a journey into the gas chambers. After this experience, she became quiet.

Once again, we called upon these beings and their help. Was there anything else that Mary had to see? This time she was shown a scene during World War One, where she was a message runner in the trenches. She remembered how much she had missed her parents whilst serving in that war, a war in which she died. The white being returned again. It asked Mary if she could look at all she had re-experienced and let it go, to forgive it. She told him she could do this, how at some deep level she felt all that had happened to her was somehow right. She could not fully explain this to herself, but it just felt right to let it all go. She opened her eyes, smiled, and told me she could see perfectly again and her arm no longer hurt her. She had made a complete recovery.

It seemed to me that her refusal to look within had been reflected in her inability to see properly, perhaps her aching arm reflected her stubborn refusal to let go of her pain and be open to healing. On some level, of which she was unaware, Mary had eventually decided this was her time of healing. She realised the pain she had been carrying for so long no longer served her, and she was ready to let it go.

6. Guided Journey

Ask the client to clarify what questions need to be asked to help him or her be healed

Example: "What do I need to change in my life in order that I can be healed?"

With the client lying down in a comfortable position, guide them on a pleasant journey through nature, maybe to the sea or a mountaintop, where they will meet a guide who understands and loves them totally, with no judgement. Leave them together in silence so they can talk together. Do the journey in your own mind so you get a sense of right timing with the words you use. Encourage the client to experience all five senses. Some people find difficulty with the visual sense but can easily imagine touch, for example. At the end of the journey, again leave the client in silence with the guide, this time for about five to ten minutes.

John asked to see me about the chronic pain at the base of his neck. He was somewhat sceptical about experiencing this type of healing as he came from a scientific background. The neck pain had been present for some months and his hospital had advised a long course of physiotherapy. I explained to John that there was a part of his mind that knew exactly what the cause of his problem was. To help him to access this, I told him I would take him through a relaxation procedure and use some techniques to help him to bypass his rational mind and open to his inner wisdom.

John lay down and I made him comfortable with cushions and a blanket. Using a progressive relaxation method, I asked him to tense and release all the muscles in his body. Whilst he was doing this, I kept my hands lightly on his head as this helps me to join with the client as well as aiding their relaxation. In a previous conversation with John I had discovered he was open to working with prayer, so I asked him to say some words to indicate his willingness to receive the help that is always there and to ask for help in seeing what thoughts he needed to change to bring about healing. I joined his silent prayer with one of my own, asking that I might open myself to my own source of help and be used as a channel for healing.

We remained in silence for a few minutes whilst I continued the laying on of hands. I asked John how he was feeling and if there was anything happening for him. He told me his aunt had appeared to him and told him: "This pain in your neck is vengeance upon yourself for what you did." John told me this was not said in an accusing manner, but rather as a simple statement of fact. However, the words made no sense to him and we decided to leave this intriguing message for the moment. Although John had stressed that he had a well-developed logical, rational, and scientific mind, he also appeared to possess strong intuition. Accordingly, I felt drawn to use imagery in the form of a guided journey, to help lead him to his own source of inner wisdom.

I began the journey by asking John to visualise himself walking down a country lane on a summer's day. To encourage him to experience all his senses, I asked him to feel the road underfoot, smell the flowers, hear the sounds of nature, and observe the surroundings and the sky above him. In this manner, he became more involved with his inner world, which, in turn, loosened the hold of his rational mind. I continued to guide him on his journey in nature, sometimes stopping to enable him to study an object of interest.

The goal of this journey was to connect John with some symbolic form of his inner wisdom or guide. However, this guided journey was soon to come to an abrupt end. I had thought that I was leading him through a forest when he stated, with some irritation, that he had tried four times to enter this forest, but each time the trees would turn into a white mist and the forest would disappear.

I suggested John should accept the mist, ask for help, and continue to walk through it. As he did so, a human cell appeared in the mist surrounded by violet light. His scientific training enabled him to recognise that the cell was cancerous. Suddenly, the memory of his dying mother returned to him, accompanied by strong feelings of guilt and shame. He told me he had felt unable to cope with the situation at the time and had given over the care of his mother to his aunt: the same aunt who had appeared at the start of the session.

John began to cry tears he had been unable to shed at the time of his mother's illness. He realised he had repressed all his guilt and shame around this issue and now needed to obtain forgiveness. I encouraged him to 'invite' his mother into the session and express to her all the things he needed to say. I told John to imagine his mother was really here in the room and to speak out loud to her. When he had finished speaking, I asked him to listen to anything his mother wanted to say to him and to repeat out loud what she said. In this way John was given an opportunity to share his buried feelings with his mother and forgive himself for his past actions.[33]

Once John felt complete with his experience I asked him to return his awareness to the room we were in. He told me the pain in his neck felt much better, and he now understood the significance of his aunt's remarks. His mother had cancer of the base of the neck and John felt his repressed guilt and shame over the handling of his mother's illness was reflected in his own bodily pain occurring in the same area.

About four days later, I asked John about his neck pain and he told me the improvement had been maintained. We had both experienced a powerful example of how the guilt in our mind is reflected in our bodily condition and how the power of forgiveness can dissolve both.[34]

---

[33] See 7. Role Reversal below.

[34] Reprinted from *Healing the Cause – A Path of Forgiveness*, Michael Dawson. Findhorn Press. 1994

7. Role Reversal

The cause of a disease is often connected with a difficult relationship with someone and it is possible to invite that other person to be present symbolically at a healing session (even if they are dead) and to talk with him or her about the issue. The client should also be encouraged to listen to what the other person has to say about the situation. Through understanding the other's point of view, healing can often take place. Asking the client to speak out loud to the person – as if he or she were really present in the room – can be very powerful. Likewise, asking the invited person to talk out loud and asking the client to repeat whatever is said – so they are addressing the remarks to themselves – can produce profound insights. In this way, the client can access their inner knowing and see the situation from the other's point of view. This approach can provide the dialogue the client may have always wanted but never achieved.

(The story of John in the previous section is a good example of this method.)

8. Inner Guide Exercise

In this exercise, the therapist becomes the questioning self of the client and writes down the questions that the client is interested in exploring and/or having answered. It is important to spend some time helping the client to explore and choose their questions in order to get the very best from the session. The client is then relaxed and asked to move into the role of his or her inner guide: the inner self who knows all the answers. I find it helps to ask the client to bring their focus to a place behind their eyes and when ready to signal or ask for the first question. The therapist then reads out the questions and writes the answers down. It is important that the therapist starts each question with 'I' and the client starts each answer with 'you'.

Example:

Q1 (decided by client, but read by therapist) – "Why am I afraid of my father?"

A1 (answered by client) – "You are afraid of your father because ...."

When the therapist has finished with the last written question they can ask, "Is there anything else (name of client) needs to know?" If the client starts to answer the questions with 'I' gently remind him or her to return to using 'you'.

In one session with a client, we had spent a fruitless hour together and made little progress. However, it suddenly occurred to me to say, "If you did know the answer to this physical problem you are suffering from, what would it be?" He surprised us both by providing an illuminating answer!

It showed me once again that we all know the cause of our physical and psychological pain – if only we could allow ourselves to access it. But this implies we are ready to look at our world differently, to drop our grievances and forgive ourselves. There is a line in *A Course in Miracles* that states: "Do you prefer that you be right or happy?"[35]

When we are willing to be wrong, to take our projections off the world and take responsibility for our ills, we can then change our minds and regain our happiness and peace.

9. Dealing with Resistance

If a client is strongly resisting a healing session, you can ask him or her to work with the resistance using visualisation techniques. I say 'strongly resisting' because all clients will carry some degree of ego resistance into any healing session. After all, if there were no resistance to healing the client would already be healed. The ego will see healing as a threat and the therapist as the enemy, so you can always expect a certain amount of opposition. However, it is important to not get frustrated with the client: any sign of frustration would play straight into the hands of the ego, which thrives on confrontation. Instead, if therapists can patiently accept their client's resistance and work gently with it, then clients are given an opportunity to change their minds

---

[35] *A Course in Miracles* T-29.VII.1:9

about the value of their ego defences and choose forgiveness instead. Once again, the example of the therapist provides the opportunity for healing.

Ask the client to describe what the resistance looks and feels like. For the sake of illustration, imagine they have described it as a brick wall. You would then ask him or her to try and overcome the obstacle and you might facilitate this by asking them to visualise a ladder on the wall so they can climb up and look over the top. Or perhaps the client can take a few bricks out of the wall and see through. Discourage the client from fighting any resistance, instead help them to understand and appreciate that this resistance has been there for their protection. Behind this defence or resistance is a fear waiting to be looked at and accepted. As the client makes friends with the resistance and starts to look at the fear it has been covering, the healing will begin.

Julie described to me how several years ago she felt a close connection to Spirit. This provided an anchor in her life, an inner beacon that she had since lost contact with, and now wanted to reconnect with.

Early on in the session she said she felt very stuck and thought nothing was going to happen. I asked her where in her body she felt stuck. Julie felt the blockage was at the top of her head, saying it felt rather like a trap door, which was closed. I asked her if she wanted to open it and she replied that she did. To her amazement she found herself floating in space with silver looking beings approaching her. They wanted to talk to her. "This is a load of nonsense!" exclaimed Julie and promptly stopped the session. We chatted for a while and she decided to try again. I asked her about her statement, if it was her voice saying this is all nonsense? She replied it was not – it felt like a man's voice.

Before going any further Julie told me about a past life experience she remembered, where she and her father were male religious leaders who had displeased their tribe. As a punishment they were blindfolded, tied up and left by themselves to die in the desert. Their death was slow and painful. As they were dying she called out to the God they served to rescue them. Close to death, with all hope gone, she had cried out, "There is no God, it is all nonsense!" Realising the connection between past and current events she felt ready to try again. Entering once more through the 'trap door' in her head, she once again experienced the silver beings who wanted to counsel her. She spent about 20 minutes in the silence conversing with them. At the end of the session she felt happy that she had left behind her grievances over being abandoned and had reconnected again with her source of love and wisdom.

∞∞∞

This chapter has served as an introduction to some of the ways I have found useful in helping others to forgive. The subject of healing is covered more fully in my book *Healing the Cause – A Path of Forgiveness*, also published by Findhorn Press. Some extracts from this book can be viewed at www.healingthecause.org.uk including some additional case studies.

SUMMARY

- The peaceful presence of a therapist heals
- This presence of peace is telling the client that he or she is not being judged
- The therapist empathises with the client's strength
- Our inner guide is the therapist
- Which therapeutic technique to use is chosen by our inner guide

EPILOGUE

As we practise forgiveness peace will progressively dawn in our minds and we will remember who we really are – our spiritual reality. When our mind is sufficiently quiet, we will become aware of an inner guide, whose guiding voice will eventually become the only voice we listen to.

His voice is always with us, but through fear we blot it out. With his help, we will remove those barriers to his presence. This is the way of forgiveness. As we hold his hand, we look together, without judgement, at the contents of our mind. Here is the only cause of suffering that can ever be found. As suffering arises in our mind through contact with the world, he gently asks us to look within instead. He reminds us that the world is only a mirror to what is in our mind. What is unforgiven in our mind is seen as something fearful in the world – something to be attacked and destroyed. "Come back to the source of pain", he calls, "for only here can it be undone". "Release your blame of others, release your blame of yourselves and surrender your pain to me", he gently reminds us.

And slowly we come to learn that there is no better way than his. So little he asks of us, so much he has to give. His light slowly dawns upon our minds, our faith begins to deepen, and we grasp his hand more tightly. His way works – ours does not. Forgetting the past and letting go of the future, we begin to become content with the moment. We understand that he can safely lead us home and we no longer desire any other journey.

The dream of separation starts to fade until at last we are lifted back to the awareness of our perfect oneness and we are home at last. At the journey's end all decision-making will cease and we will know peace at last.

Appendix One

REfERENCE NOTATION SYSTEM

The following references have been used in this book for quotations taken from *A Course In Miracles*® and two related supplements:

A Course in Miracles:
> Text (T)
> Workbook (W)
> Manual for Teachers (M)

Supplements:
> Psychotherapy: Purpose, Process and Practice (P)
> The Song of Prayer (S)

Examples of this notation:

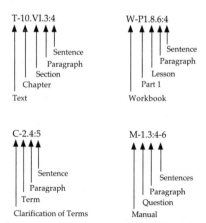

T-10.VI.3:4
- Sentence
- Paragraph
- Section
- Chapter

Text

W-P1.8.6:4
- Sentence
- Paragraph
- Lesson
- Part 1

Workbook

C-2.4:5
- Sentence
- Paragraph
- Term

Clarification of Terms

M-1.3:4-6
- Sentences
- Paragraph
- Question

Manual

Appendix Two

RECOMMENDED BOOKS & TAPES ON FORGIVENESS

BOOK AND TAPES BY MICHAEL DAWSON

Healing the Cause – A Path of Forgiveness (Book, Findhorn Press, 1994)

Identification with our body as our home is the origin of all our physical and psychological suffering. Whilst we desire to remain separate from our true spiritual identity, we create sickness to reinforce our belief in the reality of the body. To re-experience God's love, joy, and peace, we need to begin the process of forgiving ourselves and others. This will allow the presence of spirit to enter into our mind and heal it.

The cause of all disease lies in the mind and not the body. Disease is a shadow on the body of the guilt in our mind. As we practise forgiveness, the truth of who we really are will dawn upon our minds and we will discover our true home, which we never left.

Michael Dawson's inspiration for writing this book comes from his study and teaching of *A Course in Miracles*. *Healing the Cause* can also be read as an introduction to *A Course in Miracles*®, especially with regard to its teachings on sickness, healing, forgiveness and prayer.

Review of *Healing the Cause* by the Miracle Network (www.miracles.org.uk):

"Sickness, healing, forgiveness and prayer are some of the topics discussed in this book. Michael Dawson illustrates his interpretations of the Course with practical examples and diagrams. This book provides an excellent introduction to the main teachings of the Course, and will be of value to both 'new' and 'old' students of *A Course in Miracles*."

Extracts can be viewed at www.healingthecause.org.uk

Healing the Cause – Exercise series. Tapes T1 to T4

Audio tapes on healing and forgiving ourselves

Review of exercise series by Ian Patrick, Director of the Miracle Network (www.miracles.org.uk):

"This is Michael Dawson at his most down-to-earth and practical. Each of these four tapes includes two exercises, in the form of guided meditations. Most exercises begin with a relaxation process and an invitation to the Holy Spirit to enter into the situation, as the healing agent. In Michael's usual clear, concise, no-nonsense style, each exercise goes straight to the heart of the issue in question.

I found the meditations liberating, deeply healing and comforting, being based on the premise that what you accept / forgive can be released and healed – and if you're not ready to do that, that is fine too!"

T1

Side A: Self-forgiveness

Side B: Accepting and healing all aspects of ourselves

"... about accepting parts of ourselves we dislike and understanding aspects of which we are unaware."

T2

Side A: Forgiving others

Side B: Going past the illusion of sacrifice

"... helps us to heal relationships and to learn that there is no cost/ sacrifice needed to gain peace and joy."

T3

Side A: Changing your perception and finding peace

Side B: Reducing physical pain

"... returns us to the memory of who we truly are and looks at the 'message' physical pain may have for us"

T4

Side A: Changing your perceptions of another – exercise for two people

Side B: Uniting with another – exercise for two people

"...looks at how we project onto others and how we can experience the highest in them"

Taped workshops/talks on forgiveness

T5 Three Steps of Forgiveness

Concentrates on the process of forgiveness from the perspective of A Course in Miracles. Includes three healing exercises. Recorded at the Annual Miracle Network Conference in London, November 2001

T6 Summary of Forgiveness

A short summary of the three stages of forgiveness followed by an exercise on forgiveness. Recorded at the Annual Miracle Network Conference in London, November 2001

T7 Finding and eliminating the blocks to receiving guidance

This talk was recorded at the Annual Miracle Network Conference in London, October 2000

All tapes can be ordered from Michael Dawson's two websites at:
www.thecourse.org.uk or www.healingthecause.org.uk

SELECTED BOOKS AND AUDIO TAPES
BY DR. KENNETH WAPNICK

Kenneth Wapnick received his Ph.D. in psychology from Adelphi University. He worked closely with Dr. Helen Schucman and Dr. William Thetford, the two scribes of *A Course in Miracles*, and has been writing, teaching and integrating the Course's principles with his practice of psychotherapy since 1973. Ken and his wife Gloria are founders of the Foundation for *A Course in Miracles*, a teaching centre for the Course in Temecula, California. Both are writers and lecturers.

Contact details: Foundation For A Course In Miracles
41397 Buecking Drive
Temecula, CA 92590, USA
Tel: 909 296 6261 Fax: 909 296 9117
www.facim.org

Forgiveness and Jesus (book)

Addresses the misunderstandings of traditional Christianity, separating these out from the Course, and discusses the applications of the Course's principles to the major issues of our lives, such as injustice, anger, forgiveness, sickness, sexuality and money.

A Talk Given on A Course in Miracles (book)

This book provides an in-depth introduction to the principles of A Course in Miracles. It first explains the central ideas in the ego's thought system of sin, guilt, and fear, and its defences of denial and projection. Next, the Holy Spirit's thought system of forgiveness is explained, showing specifically how it and the miracle undo the ego's chief defence against the Love of God, which is the special relationship. Also included are chapters on the purpose of the life of Jesus, and the story of how the Course came to be written.

The Ego and Forgiveness (two-tape set)

An Introductory Overview of *A Course in Miracles*

The Meaning of Forgiveness (two-tape set)

Forgiveness is the central teaching of *A Course in Miracles* and has been almost universally misunderstood. In this workshop, its true meaning is explained in contrast to the distortions coming from the world's version, which has made forgiveness into a scourge rather than the path home to God. Through readings and discussion of examples, all forms of victimisation are shown to be rooted in the projection of responsibility for our belief that we are separate from God's Love. Forgiveness, therefore, begins with looking at our experiences of victimisation with Jesus, who then helps us see both their cause and their healing. These lie only in our mind's decision, either to be joined with his love or to remain separate from it.

The Simplicity of Salvation (eight-tape set)

An Intensive Overview of *A Course in Miracles*.

This workshop presents an in-depth summary of the principles of *A Course in Miracles*, with special emphasis placed on the two levels of the Course's presentation. It also includes a comparison of the Course and Christianity, and the story of how the Course was written.

MUSIC

Resta Burnham has taken many of the important themes of *A Course in Miracles* and poetically rendered them into songs, accompanied by guitar. The result is calming, healing and inspiring. Resta has made them all available for free download as mp3s from www.musicofchrist.net. Donations are appreciated, but Resta will send free CDs and lyrics to anyone who requests them. Please send requests to resta@musicofchrist.net.

Appendix Three

A COURSE IN MIRACLES AND FORGIVENESS

The inspiration for this book has come from *A Course In Miracles*. The purpose of the Course is to wake us up to our spiritual reality. This is experienced as a state of quiet joy and inner peace, which nothing in the world can take away. Through following the path of forgiveness, our mind becomes quiet, which is the required condition to remember who we really are and our oneness with all living things.

This summary will look at the origin of the Course, what the Course consists of and what it says, especially in regard to forgiveness.

ORIGIN OF THE COURSE:

The Course came as an answer to a call for help from two people, Dr. Helen Schucman and Dr. William Thetford, professors of medical psychology at Columbia University's College of Physicians and Surgeons in New York City. They worked together in a prestigious and highly academic setting. Their relationship was difficult with each often blaming the other for their own lack of peace. One day, to Helen's surprise, Bill announced, "there must be another way." He meant another way in which they could relate to each other. Helen agreed to join him to find out what this better way could be. This is an example of what the Course would call a 'Holy Instant' where, instead of seeking to separate from another, a decision is made to join in a common goal. Almost immediately, Helen began to experience a heightened awareness, highly symbolic dreams and strange images, which lasted three months and preceded the actual writing of the Course. She also started to hear an inner voice, which she knew to be Jesus. This was a further shock to Helen who described herself as an atheist. During October 1965, Jesus told Helen, "This is *A Course In Miracles*, please take notes".

Helen described this voice: "It made no sound, but seemed to be giving me a kind of rapid, inner dictation, which I took down in a shorthand notebook. The writing was never automatic. It could be interrupted at anytime and later picked up again."[36]

Helen would take down what the voice said and the following day, before work started, Bill would type it up. This process lasted seven years with the Course being published in 1976.

What the course consists of:

The Course consists of three books: Text, Workbook for Students and Manual for Teachers arranged in a self-study format. The text sets forth the thought system of the Course and is largely theoretical. The concepts in the text are practically applied through the 365 lessons of the Workbook, one for each day of the year. The Manual for Teachers provided answers to the more common questions a student might ask.

Two supplements to the Course were published later entitled Psychotherapy: Purpose, Process and Practice and The Song of Prayer.

What the course says:

The Course makes it clear that it is not the only spiritual path we should follow – There are many thousands of other forms, all with the same outcome (M.1.4). Although anyone can derive benefit from the Course, it will not appeal to everyone. It is written on a high intellectual level and for most of us, it requires a lifetime of patient study and practice.

Many Christian terms are used and there are over 700 references to the Bible. However, the Course uses many of these terms with entirely different implications. We are not depicted as sinful, guilty creatures who have displeased God and are thus worthy of punishment unless we sacrifice and atone for our sins. Instead, our sinless, formless spiritual nature is emphasised. Jesus seeks to awaken us to this truth about ourselves through his path of forgiveness.

The Course's Christian context is often a problem for students. However,

---

[36] Preface to *A Course in Miracles*.

the Course emphasises we are never upset by what we perceive in the world but only the unforgiven content of our mind that the world is mirroring back to us. In this way, we can even use the Course's language to help us with forgiveness.

A similar problem often exists for students with regard to Jesus being the author of the Course. As he says of himself:

> I am constantly being perceived as a teacher to be exalted or rejected, but I do not accept either perception of myself. .... Some bitter idols have been made of him who would be only brother to the world. Forgive him your illusions, and behold how dear a brother he would be to you.[37]

Here again we are being given an opportunity to see what the symbol of Jesus is reflecting back to us. For those wishing to explore this further please see my article *Forgiving Jesus* on www.thecourse.org.uk

The Course is written on two levels – metaphysical and practical. Metaphysics investigates what is truth and what is illusion. The following quotation is from the metaphysical level of the course:

> You dwell not here, but in eternity.
> You travel but in dreams, while safe at home.[38]

The practical teachings of the Course seek to awake us to the reality contained in that statement.

Jesus teaches us that this universe is not our real home. What is true is eternal, which means it was never born. Anything that has a beginning must have an end and as such is not real. As God is eternal so must His creations be. His creations exist outside of time and space and therefore cannot be threatened by change or death. What we mistakenly take as real changes all the time and death can strike at any moment. The Course sums this up on the first page of the Text:

> Nothing real can be threatened.
> Nothing unreal exists.
> Herein lies the peace of God.[39]

---

[37] *A Course in Miracles* T-4.I.6:7, C-5.5:7-8
[38] *Ibid.* T-13.VII.17:6-7
[39] *Ibid.* T-Introduction 2:2-4

Our true reality is really eternal, changeless, perfect formless spirit in complete oneness with God. What God did not create does not exist, apart from in a dream. In contrast, our world is one of form, bound by time, is always changing and is far from perfect. Thus God could not of made this physical universe or know of its existence. What we take as reality, this time-space world, is really a dream from which forgiveness will awaken us. Its only value is as a classroom of forgiveness.

Of course, the world does not seem like a dream to most of us. But then our dreams last night also seemed real when we were dreaming them. Why does the Course refer to the universe as a dream? The symbology of the Adam and Eve story in the Old Testament can help us here. Adam and Eve were happy in the garden (Heaven) until an idea came that perhaps things could be even better if they ate of the forbidden fruit. This fruit is described in the Course as the thought of separation and is referred to as the ego. To be separate from God and do our own thing is impossible, but to dream of it is not. In our desire for autonomy and individuality, the Course says we fell asleep so our wishes could come true in our dreams.

Into this dream, we bring fearful thoughts of what we have done to our creator. Believing we have knocked God off his throne and stolen his power has left us with a strong thought that we have sinned. This thought must leave us feeing very guilty and we expect there will be a just punishment forthcoming from God. This is depicted in Genesis as God storming into the Garden of Eden looking for the two transgressors who are trying to hide from his retribution behind a bush. On being caught, they turn to their ego's for advice on how to handle this situation. The ego's advice is, as always, to deny and project. "It's not my fault," protests Adam, "It was Eve who tempted me". "But I was persuaded by the snake" protests Eve. It's love that makes Heaven "go around" but in our dream world, it has become guilt.

Now "we travel but in dreams", forgetting we are "safe at home". We seem to have got what we wanted – separation in exchange for the oneness of God and His creation, which the Course calls the Christ. Jesus describes himself in the Course as a man who remembered he was the Christ, as we all are. The Christ shares in the love and majesty of God for there is only a perfect oneness in Heaven. Heaven cannot be understood by us who only know time and space, it has to be experienced.

In this dream, we strive to be happy believing that with enough time and opportunity the world will provide us with what we want. We say to ourselves, "If only I can find the right partner, earn enough money, maintain my health, live long, become successful in my job, and so on, then I will be happy." Even if all the conditions are met, there will always be a lurking fear in the back of our minds that any of these conditions could so easily change. The stock market could crash, our partner may get sick, war could be declared and so forth. We seem to prefer all this uncertainty to honestly saying to ourselves, "I have been wrong. There can never be any lasting peace here. Perhaps there is another way."[40] And like the prodigal son, in the end all living things will decide to return to their loving Father in Heaven.

The world we have appeared to make is based on murder. We believe, in our unconscious, we had to kill God and take His power to make our world. This thought now manifests here in our dream, as every living thing needs to kill something else to continue living and spend much of its time protecting itself or its young from being killed in turn. In the last century, over 100 million people died in wars and many more were maimed, raped, and tortured. We might say that we are vegetarians but still another life form must always die for us to continue. In contrast to Heaven (where need does not exist) ours is a world of scarcity where we fight over the resources. We need to ask ourselves the question, "Could a loving God have created such a world?"[41]

Forgiveness is the 'other way' which seeks to gently wake us from our nightmare of separation and murder and return us to the awareness of our true home in Heaven. This dream seems so real that without help we would never awaken. When the separation from God appeared to happen (it never did in reality) we took with us into the dream a memory of God (to borrow a phrase from Dr. Kenneth Wapnick) we could never quite forget. The Course calls

---

[40] *A Course in Miracles* T-30.I.12
[41] *Ibid.* T-13.in.3

this the Holy Spirit and without His help we cannot awaken. In this book, I have referred to the Holy Spirit as our inner guide.

The Holy Spirit is described as the remaining communication link between God and His separated Sons. In order to fulfil this special function the Holy Spirit has assumed a dual function. He knows because He is part of God; He perceives because He was sent to save humanity.[42]

The Holy Spirit knows the truth of our oneness with God but also recognises our illusions so that He can teach us how to overlook them. Jesus is the manifestation of the Holy Spirit and is ever present to help us with our lessons of forgiveness if we but invite him in. As Jesus has transcended his ego, his patience is infinite and he will stay with us until the end of time to help us all wake up.

After the seeming separation from God, our minds became split into three parts: the ego, the Holy Spirit and the sleeping Son of God who has to decide which of the two voices to listen to.[43] Although the Holy Spirit is always present in our minds ready to teach us another way of looking at the world, we fear to turn to Him for help. We think we have successfully abandoned God, broken up Heaven in the process, and escaped into our self-made world where He cannot find us. To have God's representative in our mind, the Voice for God, is frightening and we prefer to turn to our ego for help. "After all, does not the Holy Spirit work for God," we exclaim! "And if we turn to Him for help He will punish us for our sins".

Without the Holy Spirit's help, we are really lost as we have only the advice of the ego left. The ego is a thought we have made and, like any creation, wants to live. Its advice to us is only to ensure its own survival. Its counsel is that to escape from our dreadful feelings of guilt over the separation we need to deny the problem and project it onto the world. Until we learn to try another way we are doomed to repeat our errors. This reinforces our guilt, which in turn maintains the ego thought system. The ego's 'food' is guilt and following its advice will always lead to creating more guilt.

---

[42] *Ibid.* C-6.3:1-3
[43] Dr. Kenneth Wapnick's books and tapes deal with the split mind in great detail. See Appendix 2 for recommended books and tapes.

Although we seemed to have achieved the goal of separation and individuality we are left feeling that there is something missing in our lives, we no longer feel complete. The Holy Spirit would tell us that what is missing is the oneness with all life and God. But fearing this Voice, we have only the ego thought system to turn to. The ego tells us that there is something lacking in us and we can only find it by looking in the world for it. We try to fill the bottomless pit in ourselves by plunging into work, eating, drinking, sex, entertainment and above all by 'falling in love'. Another person or object now becomes our substitute for God – what the Course describes as a 'special love' relationship. As long as each person fulfils the needs of the other, the couple remains content for a time. But soon as one breaks this bargain, the old feeling of emptiness arises. The door over the inner pain opens again and we try desperately to close it. Our ego will counsel us to attack the other in the hope that he or she will become guilty enough to change his or her behaviour. If this fails, the relationship is likely to end and another sought instead.

At this difficult time, we could also turn to forgiveness instead of attack. The strife we are experiencing will seem all too familiar. We can ask ourselves, "Perhaps there is another way of looking at this situation. What can I lose by trying?"[44] This is an invitation to bring the power of the Holy Spirit into our minds. Our partner can be transformed from enemy to saviour becoming a mirror to our guilt. The relationship is now transformed into the goal of a holy relationship where truth and forgiveness, and not ego needs take first place. Nor does it take the other to think this way for it is our change of perception that will bring us peace. The relationship may still end but the forgiveness learnt will take us one more step to peace.

We do not have to learn about love, truth and joy for that was eternally given us and but awaits our welcome.[45] What we do need to do is to remove the blocks to that awareness and that is the role of forgiveness. Our world is a world where perception rules. (This is unknown in Heaven – in perfect oneness, there is nothing to perceive.) Our need is to correct our perception with

---

[44] *A Course in Miracles* Lesson 33
[45] *Ibid.* T-13.VII.9

the aid of the Holy Spirit or Jesus.

What we think is what we perceive. Believing separation to be real that is exactly what we perceive around us. But when we awaken from the dream and realise all is one we can only perceive everything as part of ourselves. To attack another will then be impossible, as it will seem as if we are stamping on our own feet. Everyone here perceives a different world because no two people think exactly the same. We can observe this in ourselves when we change moods. When we feel happy the world looks a far nicer place than when we are distressed.

Forgiveness teaches us that the world but reflects our thinking and therefore it is pointless to try to change the world to make ourselves happy. As I quoted earlier:

> Projection makes perception. The world you see is what you gave it, nothing more than that. But though it is no more than that, it is not less. Therefore, to you it is important. It is the witness to your state of mind, the outside picture of an inward condition. As a man thinketh, so does he perceive. Therefore, seek not to change the world, but choose to change your mind about the world.[46]

Of course, we all have our preferences with regard to clothes, climate, food, etc., which is normally linked to our conditioning. There is nothing wrong in this. However, understanding that what we perceive in the world is mirroring our state of mind is the road to lasting peace and joy. Now we have the power, with the aid of the Holy Spirit, to change our mind about the world. We realise it's foolish to blame people and circumstances for our unhappiness. Nobody and nothing has that power over us. Until this is seen we are forced to defend the world we have made up by using defence and attack. It takes a lot of work to prop up our illusions about ourselves. If we are invested in being a victim, we are forced to see a world populated by persecutors just waiting to have a go at us. Our perception of the world becomes highly selective, filtering out what does not support our beliefs and selecting that which reinforces them. Life now becomes a self-fulfilling prophecy.

---

[46] *Ibid.* T-21.in.1:1-7

Forgiveness is a process where we start to learn our perceptual errors and decide we wish to see things differently. As we correct out perceptions we begin to undo the blocks we have created and true perception or spiritual vision starts to dawn on our minds. The world we once saw as a hostile place out to attack us was but merely mirroring our own belief, that attack will get us what we want. When we think anger would get us something of value we also believe others will be thinking the same. This must result in us feeling insecure for now we are waiting to be attacked. This is why Jesus asks us to teach what we want to learn.[47]

Forgiving this false perception immediately transforms the world we live in. Now, when others attack us we can see they think like we once did and do not realise they are actually reinforcing their own sense of vulnerability. Our new perception is that their attack is a call for our help.[48] Not that they are aware of this, which does not matter, it is that we are now aware of what they are doing as we have forgiven this behaviour in ourselves. Wishing to reinforce the love we feel growing within us, we are happy to extend our love to those who attack us.

The form our behaviour will take we cannot know in advance, for what we have learned is under the direction of the Holy Spirit to which we are learning to turn more and more. If we are judged or attacked by another we may be guided to say something, to remain silent, to walk away – the appropriate loving response will be given if we are open to our inner guide.

To the ego, the body is its home. How the body looks, what others think of it becomes of prime importance. When it is sick or in pain, it is easy for us to focus on the seeming reality of the world. Now the Holy Spirit seems a liar as we say, "Don't tell me this world is not real. I am in pain!". But the body does not have a mind of its own. It must be told by the sleeping Son of God what it must feel, when it is to be born and die, whether to be sick or well. With the ego as our guide, we play the game of making our body our reality. Once we change our allegiance to the Holy Spirit, the body's function will

---

[47] *Ibid.* T-6.I.6
[48] *Ibid.* T-12.I.5

change. Now the body is perceived as a loving tool of communication instead of as a weapon of attack. This will also produce gains in vitality and health. The purpose of the body will change, no longer being seen as who we think we are. Instead, it becomes a vehicle in which we can learn our lessons in our daily classrooms of forgiveness.

How long this journey home takes is entirely up to us. All the answers to all our problems exist in this present moment, just waiting to be accepted. The Holy Spirit sees time as an illusion we have made, as we could have no separate world without it. The ego relies on its past experience to try and solve present problems, and always fails. The Holy Spirit's answers to our problems are like gifts just waiting to be unwrapped and received. We do not have to earn them or suffer or pray to receive them but simply want them with all our heart. The Holy Spirit will never go against our free will but will come instantly if He is made wholly welcome.[49] But while we think we know better and trust the counsel of our ego the gifts must wait for the day we are ready to accept them. These gifts are but various forms of forgiveness perfectly tailored to match the complexity of our problems. In time, we learn His way works and will turn more and more to Him for help.

Step by step, as we tread the path of forgiveness, we will be kindly and gently led from our nightmares to happy dreams of forgiveness.[50] The world we once perceived as dark and threatening will start to be perceived differently. Former enemies are now perceived as our saviours as they offer us the chance to forgive what we have been projecting onto them. Our days become dedicated to finding peace through forgiveness. Our bodies gain vitality as they serves a holy purpose, no longer being perceived as our identity. When all our lessons are finally learnt we will perceive the Christ in all living things. We realise that there is nothing to forgive for what God created is perfect and needs no forgiveness. Further, having left our ego behind there is nothing unhealed to project and therefore nothing to forgive.

With forgiveness complete, we enter what the Course calls 'the real

---

[49] *Ibid.* T-13.III.9
[50] *Ibid.* T-13.VII.9

world'. It is still this world but seen differently. Now we walk quietly in peace. Finding the Christ within our own mind it is now impossible to see anything else in the world. People are perceived as either giving love or asking for it.[51] This is the judgement of the Holy Spirit and so becomes ours. Whether the body lives or dies is not important. It will be known when it is time to lay it aside, just as everything else is known. Choice has gone to be replaced by an inner certainty and the need for forgiveness is over.

Appendix Four

EXERCISE IN FORGIVING OTHERS (T2A)

The following exercise can be dictated onto a tape, read to you by a friend or purchased as an audio tape [T2] – please see Appendix Two.

Introduction:
We get upset with other people because they remind us of what is unhealed, what is unforgiven in ourselves.

When this part is healed in us, we will only have compassion for their behaviour.

For example, if you find another person's anger upsetting it could be mirroring a suppressed hostility in yourself.

Remember: people you have not forgiven are mirrors of what is unforgiven in yourself

In this exercise, you will be asked at one point to welcome the help that is ever-present for all people all the time, but which we often forget is there.

This help may be known by many names: your inner guide, Higher Self, angels, Spirit, soul, Holy Spirit, God, Jesus, the Goddess. I will use the term inner guide but please feel free to use whatever name or term you feel most comfortable with.

---

[51] *Ibid.* T-12.II.1

This symbol represents a presence that is all wise and loving with absolutely no judgement of you. This presence sees what you may call 'sins' as merely nightmares which it seeks to awaken you from. It simply seeks to correct your errors of thinking and return to your memory the beauty of who you really are. It is the self you will be when you totally forgive.

Step 1: Relaxation

Make yourself comfortable, either lying or sitting (though the latter is preferable if you think you may snooze off).

• *Take some slow deep breaths.*

• *As you breathe in tense the muscles in both legs, then breathe out and release the tension.*

• *Breathe in and tense the buttocks, breathe out and release the tension.*

• *Breathe in and tense the stomach, breathe out and release the tension.*

• *Breathe in and tense the arms and fists, breathe out and release the tension.*

• *Breathe in and squeeze the shoulder blades together, breathe out and release the tension.*

• *Check that the neck is relaxed – rotate the head if necessary.*

• *Breathe in and tense the face, breathe out and release the tension.*

Count backwards from 20 to one feeling yourself becoming more relaxed as you count down.

Step 2: Asking for Help

You cannot be healed unless you accept help from what I am calling your 'inner guide'.

Send out a prayer to your inner guide in which you welcome and invite its presence to be with you. (The help is always there but needs your invitation, as it will never act against your free will.)

You may wish to imagine this help as a ray of light shining down upon you; as a presence you can feel surrounding you; or as a loving being whose hand you hold.

Step 3: Exercise

Ask your inner guide to show you someone you need to forgive.

PAUSE

Recall to mind the conversations and events connected with the person you feel disturbed about.

PAUSE

If strong feelings of anger arise say what you need to say to the person (for instance, unexpressed thoughts and feelings), it is all right to feel angry or upset.

PAUSE

Feel in your body where you are holding feelings and emotions connected with this person.

PAUSE

Place your hand over the area of discomfort.
Say to yourself "I accept these feelings of .... They are part of me."
Repeat the sentence until you feel more comfortable with these emotions.

PAUSE

Now imagine the person is standing in front of you.
If this feels threatening to you, see him or her as a small distressed child who, like you, is trying to cope with life's challenges.
See the person change into a full-length mirror and see your image there.
Ask your inner guide to explain to you:
– In what way is my behaviour similar to this person?
– Am I capable of similar behaviour, albeit in a different form?
– What is this relationship teaching me?

PAUSE

Become aware of any remaining pain you may be feeling around this issue.
Tell yourself it no longer serves you to hold onto it.
Ask now for help and open to the light of your inner guide.
See/feel the light around you.

PAUSE

Imagine yourself opening that part of your body where you feel the pain to the presence of the light.
Feel the light pour in and lovingly surround the pain.
With each breath that you take, you draw the love of your inner guide into your pain.
Release any judgement you hold about your pain and ask the inner guide to transmute and heal it.

PAUSE

Your pain is your gift to the guide, which it will joyously take away.
Continue until you feel complete.

PAUSE

Once again, see/feel the person you wish to forgive.
Become aware of their fear and pain and see it as a call for your love.
You understand how their fear and pain makes them behave as they do.
Say anything you need to them – as if that person were standing in front of you. If you wish, say it out loud.

PAUSE

Listen to anything they may need to say to you. If you want you can become that person and speak out loud to yourself

PAUSE

Thank the person for being your teacher.

Appendix Five

FORGIVENESS EXERCISE (T3A)

Changing your perception and finding peace

The following exercise can be dictated onto a tape, read to you by a friend or purchased as an audio tape [T3] – please see Appendix Two.

Introduction:

This is a short exercise to do any time you feel threatened or disturbed by others, or a particular situation.

In this exercise, you will be asked at one point to welcome the help that is ever-present for all people all the time, but which we often forget is there.

This help may be known by many names: inner guide, Higher Self, angels, Spirit, soul, Holy Spirit, God, Jesus, the Goddess.

I will use the term inner guide but please feel free to use whatever name or term you feel most comfortable with.

This symbol represents a presence that is all wise and loving with absolutely no judgement of you. This presence sees what you may call 'sins' as merely nightmares which it seeks to awaken you from. It simply seeks to correct your errors of thinking and return to your memory the beauty of who you really are. It is the self you will be when you totally forgive.

Step 1: Relaxation

Make yourself comfortable, either lying or sitting (though the latter is preferable if you think you may snooze off).

• Take some slow deep breaths.

• As you breathe in tense the muscles in both legs, then breathe out and release the tension.

• Breathe in and tense the buttocks, breathe out and release the tension.

• Breathe in and tense the stomach, breathe out and release the tension.

• Breathe in and tense the arms and fists, breathe out and release the tension.

• Breathe in and squeeze the shoulder blades together, breathe out and release the tension.

• Check that the neck is relaxed – rotate the head if necessary.

• Breathe in and tense the face, breathe out and release the tension.

Count backwards from 20 to one feeling yourself becoming more relaxed as you count down.

Step 2: Asking for Help

You cannot be healed unless you accept help from what I am calling your 'inner guide'.

Send out a prayer to your inner guide in which you welcome and invite its presence to be with you. (The help is always there but needs your invitation, as it will never act against your free will.)

You may wish to imagine this help as a ray of light shining down upon you; as a presence you can feel surrounding you; or as a loving being whose hand you hold.

Step 3: Exercise

(thanks go to my friend, Lee Oldershaw, who received in meditation the idea for this part of the exercise)

Think of someone you are having a problem with in your life, someone with whom you have some unresolved issue. Bring to mind the last difficult situation.

Become aware of the feelings that you are experiencing and notice where they are located in the body.

This is the part in you that stores the same or similar behaviour, albeit in a different form.

What does that part of you look like?

Ask your inner guide for a symbol or picture that represents it.

Just let the picture come by itself spontaneously.

Decide if you want to keep this symbol or whether you would rather heal and transmute the symbol.

If you want to heal it, ask to be given another symbol and let the new symbol appear and grow in front of you.

Just observe it.

What has it changed into? What does it look like?

Decide if you want to keep this symbol and allow it to replace the old one.

Now see the person that you projected onto in front of you, and give them this new symbol as a gift.

See their happiness on receiving it.

This person has been a teacher for you and this is your gift to them.

Say whatever you need to say to them and listen to what they may have to say to you. Try to recognise that your similarities, mirrored back to you, are causing the pain.

Thank the person for the lesson you are learning from them.

Appendix Six

FORGIVENESS EXERCISE (T4B)

Uniting with another (for two people)

The following exercise can be dictated onto a tape, read to you by a friend or purchased as an audio tape [T4] – please see Appendix Two.

Introduction:

The purpose of this exercise is to help you unite with another person, to go beyond the barriers of ego, of personality and reach out to oneness of spirit that we all are.

In this exercise, you will be asked at one point to welcome the help that is ever-present for all people all the time, but which we often forget is there.

This help may be known by many names: inner guide, Higher Self, angels, Spirit, soul, Holy Spirit, God, Jesus, the Goddess.

I will use the term inner guide but please feel free to use whatever name or term you feel most comfortable with.

This symbol represents a presence that is all wise and loving with absolutely no judgement of you. This presence sees what you may call 'sins' as merely nightmares which it seeks to awaken you from. It simply seeks to correct your errors of thinking and return to your memory the beauty of who you really are. It is the self you will be when you totally forgive.

Step 1: Relaxation

Sit opposite your partner and close your eyes.

* *Take some slow deep breaths.*
* *Breathe in and tense both legs, breathe out and release the tension.*
* *Breathe in and tense the buttocks, breathe out and release the tension.*
* *Breathe in and tense the stomach, breathe out and release the tension.*
* *Breathe in and tense the arms and fists, breathe out and release the tension.*
* *Breathe in and squeeze the shoulder blades together, breathe out and release the tension.*
* *Check that the neck is relaxed – rotate the head if necessary.*
* *Breathe in and tense the face, breathe out and release the tension.*

Count backwards from 20 to one feeling yourself becoming more relaxed as you count down.

Step 2: Asking for Help

You cannot be healed unless you accept help from what I am calling your 'inner guide'.

Send out a prayer to your inner guide in which you welcome and invite its presence to be with you. (The help is always there but needs your invitation, as it will never act against your free will.)

You may wish to imagine this help as a ray of light shining down upon you; as a presence you can feel surrounding you; or as a loving being whose hand you hold.

Step 3: Exercise

Let your eyes gently open now, to naturally and easily meet the eyes of your partner. Look deeply into each other's eyes.

Become aware of their personality, their age, sex, physical characteristics, any pain, or fear you might see or sense through their eyes.

Allow these things you are aware of to gradually subside and concentrate on your partner's eyes.

See the depth in those eyes.

Go deeper into them and begin to see the light in your partner's eyes.

There is a spark of divinity there.

Allow yourself to see this or sense it.

Close your eyes now and mentally picture the light you saw or could sense in your partner's eyes.

If you did not see or sense this light, just know that it is there.

Begin to visualise or feel this light as a brilliant ball and know that your own light is the same: a brilliant ball of light that is the divinity within you.

This light represents who you really are, one with your partner, one with spirit, with God.

As you visualise or feel your own light and that of your partner, see or sense these two lights in your mind's eye, these two lights emerging from each other's body and then coming together, merging into each other.

See or sense these two separate lights fusing into each other, becoming one light. Become aware of the power of this, the beauty, and the freedom.

And if there is any resistance or fear, just observe it, allowing it to be there.

The light begins to move upwards now, rising higher and higher, joined together as one light and gently, gradually, moving into the pure vastness beyond matter.

Peace is all around you, you feel free and open.

Now see yourself approaching a vast expanse of light, the sky is nothing but light.

You feel the brilliance of your own joined light, but the light you are entering becomes stronger and stronger until it is the same brilliance as your own light.

You feel your own light, two souls joined together merging with this other light.

You feel your boundaries gently fading away as you become one with this vast being of light.

Here you are joined in eternity: formless, changeless, perfect, and limitless.

You are peace, compassion, love, and truth – take a moment to feel this, to experience it. Allow Spirit to be with you in the silence.

PAUSE for a few minutes here.

Begin to bring your awareness back.

Feel yourself coming back into the room.

Open your eyes and look into the eyes of your partner.

Just let your eyes meet softly, gently, no strain, just being, feeling what is flowing between you.

Reach out now and take each other's hands – continue to keep the eye contact in silence.

When you feel ready, take a moment to share with each other your experiences.